MOB HIT ON MY GRANDMOTHER'S DOG

Funny Animal Stories to Make You Laugh, Chortle, Snicker and Feel Inspired

Edited by Matt Jackson

Summit Studios

Library and Archives Canada Cataloguing in Publication

Mob hit on my grandmother's dog : funny animal stories to make you laugh, chortle, snicker and feel inspired / edited by Matt Jackson.

Issued in print and electronic formats.
ISBN 978-0-9866856-3-7 (pbk.).--ISBN 978-0-9866856-4-4 (html).--ISBN 978-0-9866856-5-1 (pdf)

1. Animals--Humor. 2. Canadian wit and humor (English). I. Jackson, Matt, editor

PN6231.A5M63 2014   C818'.602080362   C2014-903980-8
C2014-903981-6

Designed by Kirk Seton, Signet Design Inc.
Printed and bound in Canada

SUMMIT STUDIOS
3022 Washington Ave.
Victoria, British Columbia V9A 1P6

This book is dedicated to all those

who love animals.

Table of Contents

Introduction

By Matt Jackson

When Summit Studios first released *Mugged by a Moose* in 2006—the first volume of our travel and outdoor humor series—I could not have guessed that it would be so well received. Stephen Leacock aside, the market for humor books in Canada is not a large one. It's tiny, actually. And while modern scribes such as Stuart McLean and Will Ferguson (both of them winners of the Leacock Medal for Humour) might be household names, I had reservations about whether there would be a market for a compilation from up-and-coming writers.

As it turned out, there was.

Seven years and six travel and outdoor humor anthologies later we have finally decided to branch out—to till our literary garden, so to speak. In January 2012 we ran a story contest where we invited writers to send us their humorous stories with some different themes. Over the next few years, assuming that all goes according to plan, we hope to release a much wider range of humor-themed books. Laughter is one language that's understood around the world.

The idea for the anthology you're now holding in your hands came to me when a friend sheepishly admitted that he was addicted to watching funny cat videos on the Internet. "Cat videos? Really?" I said. But when I began to think about it, I realized that hardly a day goes by when I haven't seen or read an online "news story" about some mischievous or funny animal. Stories about dogs and cats, not surprisingly, always seem to rank near the top of the list.

How can this be?

It's because animals can be hilarious. Pets are also those (mostly) judgment-free companions who love their owners unconditionally. When these same animals demonstrate human traits—particularly the ability to think for themselves (or better yet, get themselves into trouble)—is it surprising that they make us laugh? All the better that laughing does nothing to hurt their canine or feline feelings. We don't even have to feel guilty about it!

There are of course as many different types of animals as there are stories about them. This collection features four basic categories. The first type showcases amusing tales about pets such as cats, dogs, birds, monkeys—and yes, even a pet wasp. The story about the "pet wasp" was penned by Ilonka Halsband of Moose Jaw, Saskatchewan, and incidentally was one of the prizewinners in our 2012 short story contest.

The second type of story can loosely be categorized as stories from the farm. Ranging from tales about Alan Longworth's "near-death experiences" while growing up on a farm with three brothers, to Lois Gordon's transition from living in Toronto to subsisting amidst the green fields and meadow muffins seventy kilometers north of the city, these odes to rural life are sure to bring a smile to the faces of those familiar with country life. Not to mention the offbeat story of Sylvia Shawcross's "type-three" friend Frederick, who despite the protestations of his unenthusiastic host, is bent on learning how to butcher, clean, and cook a chicken that he stole from a pigeon hawk.

We also have a few stories about wild animals and their interactions with humans. Case in point: Carolyn Kohler and her husband Tom meet a bear in California's Ansel Adams Wilderness that possesses a rather peculiar set of skills, while Madge Brown—a former campground attendant in Banff National Park—is forced to intervene when a woman tries to get into fisticuffs with a grizzly bear that's raiding the picnic table in her campsite.

And finally, there are those stories that defy easy categorization, such as the prize-winning story written by humorist Steve Pitt. Just how does one classify a yarn that features a lobster, a marching band, and a date with Queen Elizabeth?

The stories mentioned here are but a few of the many, and I hope you will enjoy reading the book as much as I've enjoyed editing it. Moreover, if you have a story of your own that you feel deserved to appear in this collection, I hope you'll send it to us so that we can consider sharing it in a future volume.

The Queen

A lobster, a marching band, and a date with her royal nibs. Need we say more?

By Steve Pitt

Back in 1971, I had a date with the Queen. Elizabeth II. She was coming to open the Ontario Legislature and I was a member of the forty-eighth Highlanders of Canada, her official honor guard. It was one of those freakishly hot Black-Hole-of-Calcutta days for which Toronto is famous. Temperatures hovered in the high nineties (that's the mid thirties for you non-Fahrenheit kids out there) and we were about to march a mile in full uniform, which included ten pounds of wool kilt, winter-weight scarlet tunic, and a Victorian monstrosity of headgear called a feather bonnet.

The feather bonnet resembles an "I tot I taw a Puddy Tat, Tweety" style birdcage swallowed whole by a feather boa. If that isn't ridiculous enough, sometime back in the 1880s some military fop added four long black tentacles that hang down the right side of the bonnet so that the hat looks like some sort of maimed tarantula. The only good thing about those "legs" is that they conceal a fist-sized space inside which one can store one's white gloves, handkerchiefs, caviar-flavored breath mints, and other essentials one might need on a date with the Queen.

Minutes before the parade began, one of the junior officers we call Sugarbear had a sudden brainstorm. He decided to bring a small frozen cooler pack that he intended to place in his feather bonnet for the march. "You slobs are going to bake. Me, I've got air conditioning," bragged Sugarbear.

But he made the mistake of leaving his feather bonnet unattended in the Officers' Mess Hall, and two corporals (we won't say who) switched Sugarbear's cold pack for a dead raw lobster that we (I mean they) found curled up in an ice-filled catering cooler left over from an officers' banquet the previous night. The corporals took the lobster out, wrapped it in paper towels so that it mimicked the ice pack, and placed it in Sugarbear's bonnet. Then they flipped a coin for the ice pack. I lost.

The parade began. With great pomp and ceremony, the armory doors opened. To the skirl of their world-famous pipes and drums, the forty-eighth Highlanders of Canada marched out into the noonday sun, applauded by half a dozen derelicts and some morning-shift prostitutes who habitually shared our corner of Queen and Jarvis. The neighborhood improved as we marched west down Queen Street to the Eaton Centre and hooked up with the Governor General's Horse Guards, who because of military tradition were allowed to march in front of us. Thousands of people were now lining University Avenue. Time to stand up and march proud.

Bagpipes seem to work on horses the way prune juice works its way through one's bowels. As we turned up University, the horses began dropping manure mines that we, in our white spats, had no choice but to march through. Fortunately, I happened to be at the front of my column, so I saw the turds as they fell and could make delicate little sashays to keep my spats clean. The poor chumps behind me, however, had no such luck. Over the screech of bagpipes and the cheering of royalty-crazed and applauding spectators, I could hear a steady stream of multilingual curses as my fellow Highlanders stamped and punted steaming fresh horse piles in every direction.

I was so preoccupied dodging poop petards that I almost didn't notice a long green antenna emerge from between the spider legs of Lieutenant Sugarbear's feather bonnet. It was followed by a large green claw. It turns out the lobster wasn't dead after all; it had just gone into cryogenic hibernation in the catering cooler. Having escaped a knife through the brain or a pot of boiling water, the lobster was enjoying its honored position. The claw seemed to address the crowds by rotating in a perfect Royal Family Wave as we turned left off University to take our post in front of the legislature. The pipe band climbed up the steps and we formed up in three ranks as Her Royal Nibs rolled up in a horse-drawn coach.

Or that was the plan. Some hitch in timing had us standing at attention for fifteen minutes in the full sun with no Queen in attendance. With the sun's rays bouncing off the pink sandstone of the legislature and the fresh black pavement, it felt as if we were standing on a broiler rack. All around me, Highlanders were beginning to wobble like bowling pins in a breeze as they struggled to stay conscious. The only thing that kept me from falling was the sight of the lobster claw waving in smaller and smaller circles, only to slump and finally sink into Sugarbear's feather bonnet. I felt ready to follow.

A piper passed out and began rolling down the legislature steps, his pipes making a pathetic *waaaaa waaaaa waaaaa* noise each time he rolled over them. He finally came to rest facedown at the bottom of the steps, kilt over his head, Irish Republic orange-and-green boxers in full display. The male nurses from the nearby medical corps tent swooped in and carried him away. That was the last straw for the Colonel. Against orders, he commanded us to stand at ease and then stand easy.

We had about two seconds to enjoy our rest before the clatter of horse hooves indicated that the Queen was about to arrive.

We snapped to at ease, and then to attention, just as the gilded carriage rolled up with the Queen, Prince Phillip, the Premier, the Mayor, and the Lieutenant Governor General all aboard. The marching band struck up. Ten thousand spectators applauded. I'm not sure if it was the combined movement of hands, but a slight wind began to stir. Suddenly, I could smell the scent of fresh cut lawn, the combined sweaty nether regions of a hundred and twenty men dressed in heavy wool and ostrich feathers, horse excrement ... and seafood.

The Queen stepped down from the carriage, followed by her posse. We presented arms. The Queen indicated that she would like to inspect us. We were ordered into open order formation. I was in the second rank so it took about ninety seconds for the Queen to pass. I was so intent on standing perfectly at attention that I almost missed her. Since childhood I have become accustomed to looking *up* at the Queen, because her portrait was always mounted high on a wall in every public school, bank, or public building that I've visited. I was expecting a six-foot-six Warrior Amazon Queen. Turns out she's just a wee thing. Eyes lifted, I just barely managed to see a yellow pillbox hat pass under my nose, followed by Prince Phillip's gargoylian profile. The smell of ostrich-steamed lobster continued to waft on the breeze. Phillip caught a sniff. His perplexed expression seemed to say, "Bloody colonials."

Inspection over, we closed ranks and stood at ease while the Queen made a speech at the podium. With the Queen's back turned, Highlanders began dropping like ripe fruit. The medical corps male nurses, usually ignored, were having a feeding frenzy on prostrate Highlanders. The newspaper photographers moved in and tried to take embarrassing photographs. Shutters were snapping and the thought of seeing our pictures in the next day's newspaper—being dragged off by medical orderlies—made each one of us determined not to fall. But there was no mercy from that sun. I began seeing black spots in front of my face and was about to barf on the man in front of me, so I went down on one knee for just a few seconds. My head quickly cleared, but just as I was about to stand up again, two pairs of strong hands seized me by the arms.

"Come along," the nurses whispered.

"Back off. I'm fine," I said.

"No, no. You need some lemonade," the medical orderly insisted.

I was about to tell him where to cram his lemonade when we heard a loud *SMACK!* Lieutenant Sugarbear had passed out in perfect highland form, his sporran hitting the pavement with a click, followed by his sword rattling across the pavement.

"Ooh, he's a big one," one of the nurses said. They dropped me to score the trophy roadkill.

I could see their noses wrinkle as they approached the downed officer. They looked around for the source of the foul stench.

When they couldn't find it, they merely shrugged and carried Sugarbear away.

Several minutes later, our fallen comrades discretely rejoined us as the Queen stepped off the podium to accept some flowers from several kindergarten students.

"Have a nice nap?" the company sergeant major asked Sugarbear, handing him his claymore sword, which was going to cost him a hundred and twenty beers for dropping once we all got back to the armories.

Lieutenant Sugarbear didn't answer. He didn't seem to care about beer. Instead, he swept the lot of us with a "which-one-of-you-idiots?" cold stare. That's when one's military training comes in handy: eyes front, deadpan face, no giggling. As we marched home I wondered if Sugarbear had shared his lobster with the medical corps nurses. I imagined it went well with the lemonade.

*Steve Pitt has been a professional writer for more than thirty-five years. In 1980 he won a Periodical Distributors Author's Award for humor for an article that appeared in Harrowsmith magazine. He is the author of eight books and many hundreds of magazine articles. In addition to being a writer, Steve Pitt has worked as a movie extra, army reserve soldier, dishwasher, farmhand, martial arts instructor, bartender, youth outreach worker, armored truck guard, Yukon gold prospector, manager of a shelter for homeless men, goose rancher, lay minister, bar bouncer, resort cook, and stay-at-home dad. You'll find him in cyberspace at **www.stevepitt.ca.***

Izzy

She was a rather unusual pet.

By Ilonka Halsband

My husband Joe had a hernia repaired recently. While the procedure has been radically simplified over the years, one rule remains the same: no lifting for six weeks after the operation.

Though retired, Joe has always been an active man. On any given day he'll mow the lawn, dig up a flowerbed, change a tire, lift a barge, or tote a bale. I knew that life without lifting was going to be a challenge for him.

In the week following his surgery he sorted five years' worth of pre-digital photos into chronological order, matched up all his stray socks, sorted the books in my home office by size, and color-coded his closet. In the second week he discovered the washer; he called me at work to ask if he could put a blue rayon shirt in a load with blue jeans. I took an early lunch and went home to hide my laundry.

There were pluses to having Joe temporarily on the injured list. The bed was made, our floors were mopped, and most nights I arrived home to find dinner on the table.

In week four, Joe's convalescence took a surreal turn. That Friday evening, when I came through the door, I found him arranging an attractive assortment of appetizers on the patio table.

"I could get used to this," I said, dipping a shrimp in cocktail sauce and accepting a glass of Chenin Blanc.

Joe smiled, but he seemed a bit preoccupied as he surveyed the backyard. I assumed he was lamenting the scraggly condition of the lawn and pining for the day he could cut the grass again. I reached for a cracker and smeared it with Brie. Joe took a shrimp and laid it on the deck railing.

I paused in mid crunch and considered my husband, expecting an explanation. None came. Instead, he launched into a description of how he planned to relocate our storage shed to the far corner of the lawn once the ban on lifting was removed.

"OK," I said, as a wasp zoomed in and landed on the shrimp Joe had placed on the railing. "But you'll get some help, right? You don't want another hernia." I waved my hand over the shrimp, shooing the wasp away.

"Don't!" Joe shouted. "That's Izzy!"

I gave myself a moment. Joe has been stern and he has been firm, but in twenty-one years of marriage he has never actually shouted—at least not at me.

"Izzy?"

"The wasp," he said. "She's tame. I call her Izzy. She's been around all afternoon. That's her third shrimp."

"You're feeding shrimp to wasps?"

"Just Izzy," he said. "Not the interlopers."

"Interlopers?"

"The others."

I drank some wine. Izzy returned. At least I presumed it was

Izzy because Joe smiled fondly as she settled on the shrimp and went about gnawing herself off a slab. It was not an easy task, requiring no less than six changes of position. But eventually she liberated a piece about the size of a large peppercorn—from Izzy's perspective, equal to a side of beef. I watched, fascinated, as she attempted to take flight. The weight of her trophy caused her to plunge an alarming distance from the deck railing before she stabilized the load and zipped away.

"She must be Xena of the wasp world," I said.

Joe beamed proudly. I made a mental note to research unusual side effects of hernia surgery.

Moments later the wasp returned and circled the seafood on the railing. She hovered briefly before choosing a place to land. Joe flapped both hands over the shrimp until the wasp lost interest and flew away.

"Interloper," he explained.

"How do you know?" I asked. I couldn't help myself.

"Izzy never hesitates. She just drops in, chews off a slice, then takes it straight home."

Some minutes later another wasp arrived and performed as Joe had described, zeroing in for a perfect landing and immediately going to work. By sunset all that remained of the shrimp was the tail shell.

The next day Izzy was the only one treated to appetizers, and by the end of week five the cocktail ring was half gone and Joe's Izzy obsession had escalated.

"She recognizes me," he said one evening. "She's waiting for me when I go outside."

"And the interlopers?" I asked.

"They don't come around much anymore," he said. "They know I'll run them off."

Try as I might, I had a hard time imagining my husband—a retired RCMP officer—sitting shotgun over a chewed up chunk of seafood so his pet wasp could become the pride of the nest.

"Wouldn't you like to do some laundry tomorrow?" I asked.

Joe's Izzy fixation eventually faded when, after week six, his doctor declared him healthy and removed the restriction on lifting. By the following Friday the yard was restored to manicured perfection, the backyard fence was newly stained, and dinner preparation once again became my responsibility.

To celebrate the return to normalcy I assembled a tray of Joe's favorite appetizers, including several plump jumbo shrimp. We snacked, sipped wine, and enjoyed the late summer sunshine in companionable silence.

Moments later a wasp zoomed in for a perfect three-point landing on the half-eaten shrimp left on my plate. Joe rolled up the Canadian Tire flyer he'd been browsing and smashed the insect into mush.

My jaw dropped. "Wasn't that Izzy?"

"Couldn't be," he said. "Wasps only live a couple of weeks." He dropped the flyer to the deck. "How'd you like a gazebo in the south corner of the yard?"

I considered the wasp smear on my plate. "Could you make it a screen house?"

Ilonka Halsband lives in Moose Jaw, Saskatchewan, where she serves on the board of the Saskatchewan Festival of Words. When not chronicling husband Joe's wacky antics, Ilonka collects anecdotes about uncommon methods of murder, which she incorporates into her mystery novels. Her most recent novel was short-listed for the 2013 Crime Writers of Canada's "Unhanged Arthur" Award.

Mob Hit on My Grandmother's Dog

One surefire way to make it onto Santa's naughty list.

By Matt Jackson

A few years after my paternal grandfather passed on, there was an opportunity for my grandmother Clara to own a small Pomeranian named Sam. The family that owned him had several small children who—being children—loved to play with the dog. However, their idea of gentle play was often quite different than Sam's idea. After an incident where Sam nipped at one of his small "adversaries," the family felt that it was time to send the six-year-old Pom to a less stressful home.

My father, Bud, felt that if my grandmother had a small dog in the house it would help to keep her company. My dad was an only child who had moved our family to Ontario for work when I was fifteen, and because my grandmother lived several thousand kilometers away in Edmonton, Alberta, it was difficult for us to see her as often as we would have liked. When my father asked my grandma if she wanted Sam as a pet—and showed her a picture of the smiling, tuft-eared dog—she was very excited.

"I'll call him Poopsie," she said.

"Actually, he already has a name," said my father. "It's Sam."

"Does he *look* like Sam to you?" said my grandmother. "His name is Poopsie."

My grandmother and Poopsie quickly became best of friends. She would take the dog for "walkies" at least twice a day, and he was well fed—not only with dog food, but with countless morsels of tasty table scraps. There was a veritable conveyor belt of food that found its way from my grandmother's plate into Poopsie's stomach.

A veterinarian who ran a clinic two blocks from my grandma's home repeatedly warned my grandmother not to feed Poopsie from the table. "It's not healthy for him to eat people-food," she said. "He'll get sick."

But my grandmother couldn't seem to resist Poopsie's plaintive, melancholy eyes, because she continued feeding him table scraps despite the warnings. Within months he looked like a furry balloon with a face, tail, and stubby little legs that seemed barely capable of carrying his weight.

When Poopsie barked, my grandmother always assumed that he needed to use the doggie facilities, so she would chant, "Poopsie go pee-pee, Poopsie go pee-pee," as she let him out the screen door at the back of her condominium. Whether or not Poopsie actually used the facilities during these short excursions into nature is a question for debate, for it didn't prevent him from peeing and pooping on my grandmother's carpet on a regular basis. I suppose he was just living up to his namesake.

During the first couple of visits after Poopsie arrived, my father and I tried to train him so that he would only do his business when he was outside. But this was extremely difficult because—even if we raised our voices at Poopsie only slightly, to indicate that peeing in the middle of the living room carpet was *not* OK—my grandmother would tear a strip off of us. She would not tolerate anybody scolding her dear Poopsie, and no measure of explanation was going to change her mind. She would gladly clean up his "accidents," thank you very much, and that was all there was to it!

Poopsie was also a fairly high-strung little dog, and it was easy to see why he'd found it difficult living amidst a flock of small children. Whenever somebody knocked at my grandmother's front door—or if there was any kind of noise that Poopsie didn't recognize—he would quickly work himself into a lather. He would run around the condominium like a miniature tornado while barking at the top of his lungs, until the person (or noise) eventually went away. My grandmother didn't particularly like this behavior, but she would have forgiven Poopsie any transgression.

Despite Poopsie's imperfections, my grandmother really did seem to perk up after he came into her life—and for that we were all grateful.

In December 2001, my father unexpectedly passed away. By this time I was living in Canmore, Alberta—about a five-hour drive from where my grandmother lived—so I was the family member best able to take over the many tasks my father had been trying to do from a distance. By this time, both my grandma and Poopsie had some serious health issues. Two years earlier my grandmother had suffered a mild stroke, something she had not fully recovered from. Then, a month after my father passed on, she was diagnosed with dementia. We had suspected this for some time, but the three physicians that I visited with her all confirmed it. Every one of them told me that she would have to move into some kind of care facility; Meals on Wheels and regular visits from family and friends were no longer going to cut it.

For his part, Poopsie was twelve years old and had developed cataracts in both eyes. He was also diabetic and required an insulin shot every day. On weekdays, my grandmother still walked the two blocks to her local veterinary clinic so that Poopsie could have his daily injection. But on weekends and holidays I had to arrange special visits by a vet who did house calls, which was both expensive and logistically difficult to arrange on those weekends when the traveling vet was not available.

Meanwhile, I began searching Edmonton for care facilities—a task that proved more difficult than I had anticipated. Part of the problem was that my grandmother refused to move. I tried talking with her about it, cajoling her into looking at different options, and on one occasion I even took her to see one of the care homes without telling her what we were doing. I figured that if she liked the food and atmosphere, she might be more inclined to discussing the topic. When she realized what was going on, however, she got up from the meal and walked out the front door, then proceeded to tear a strip off me as we drove home. I knew that it was the dementia talking, but it was still not easy to witness this transition in someone who I had always loved so much.

The other problem was finding a facility that would consider taking Poopsie to ease my grandmother's transition—even for a short period of time. In fact, I was only able to find one place that met all of my criteria: it was friendly and well kept, it had decent-sized private apartments and good food, and it was reasonably affordable. Moreover, although it had a no-pet policy, the building manager offered to bend the rules for the first month while my grandmother became accustomed to living there. I felt certain that once my grandma had adjusted, I would be able to take Poopsie until he had lived out the remainder of his life—which considering his poor condition would not be long.

I asked my mom to fly out from Toronto on the week of the move. My grandma didn't know what was happening, and I wanted another family member there to help console her when the moving company arrived, especially since I would likely be distracted with the logistics of the actual move.

To our collective surprise, my grandmother adjusted to the care home very quickly. I'm sure it helped to have Poopsie there. By the third day she was happily sitting in the dining room awaiting dinner, chatting amicably with the other residents sitting at her table. My mom and I were very relieved.

Unfortunately, the care facility did not adjust to Poopsie quite so well. Mrs. Jones, who lived in the room directly across from my grandmother's apartment, felt like her world had been turned upside down. Whenever my grandma wasn't in her room—and sometimes even when she was—Poopsie would stand at the door and bark in his yappy little Pomeranian voice. Eventually Mrs. Jones could stand it no more, and she asked her church reverend to pay a visit to John, the facility's manager. Even though John assured them that Poopsie was a temporary guest, it was clear they were not happy. They threatened to move out if the dog wasn't gone by the end of the month.

There was also the difficulty of cleaning up after Poopsie. Doing so in my grandmother's apartment was one thing, but Poopsie had a knack for leaving deposits along the facility's carpeted hallways and inside the elevator. On more than one occasion residents who clearly hadn't seen the deposits pushed their walkers through them, which effectively smeared dog excrement up and down the hallways.

John called and pleaded with me to take Poopsie as soon as possible. "He's not working out very well," he admitted.

In early December, three weeks after my grandmother had moved in, I drove back to Edmonton to explain that Poopsie could no longer stay at the care home. Since I was also living in a pet-free apartment, my mother had graciously agreed to take Poopsie until he was ready to make the trip up to doggie heaven. I knew that my grandmother would be extremely sad, and no doubt emotional, but I figured that I could take her shopping for a budgie or hamster or some other pet that didn't grease the hallways with poop or give poor Mrs. Jones heart palpitations. What I had not anticipated was my grandmother—who had always been a tiny sprite of a thing— picking up one of her metal kitchen chairs and trying to hit me with it.

She was furious!

I tried to reason with her, but she would not calm down and would not be reasoned with. I envisioned the homicide unit of the Edmonton police department trying to identify my remains should I attempt to pry the dog from her white-knuckled grasp. More accurately, I was deeply concerned for her mental well-being should I take the dog from her by force. I was one of the few human "lifelines" she had left in the world, and I did not know how she would respond if she identified me as Public Enemy Number One. I recalled the time that she had lost her driver's license. She had blamed it on my father, even though he had nothing to do with it. She had failed a vision test and had her license revoked by the transport ministry; my grandmother had accused my father of calling the ministry ahead of time and asking them to revoke it. She remembered my father's "involvement" for years after the fact, and I don't think she ever entirely forgave him.

To say that I was stressed when I spoke to John about the situation is an understatement. John was a fine person and a true gentleman, and he had been very kind to temporarily bend the rules for my grandmother's sake. Nevertheless, he did not take it well when I asked him for an extension. He told me that Mrs. Jones had been stirring up a hornet's nest of controversy, and that he was likely to lose several tenants on the sixth floor if Poopsie was not removed posthaste.

"I don't know what to tell you, John," I said. "You should have seen the look on my grandma's face when I tried to take Poopsie from her. It could kill her."

"I appreciate that," he said. "But the dog can't stay here. None of the other residents like him."

"I know he can't. I just need a couple of weeks to figure out what to do."

John was not happy, but eventually he relented. "Two weeks," he said. "That's it."

On the drive back to Canmore, I thought long and hard about what to do. The only reasonable solution I could come up with was to have somebody sneak up to my grandmother's apartment while she was having lunch and put the dog to sleep—a mob hit, if you will. If the assassin arranged Poopsie in his little doggie bed just so, it would look like he had simply drifted off in his sleep. My grandmother could mourn for him, give him a proper burial, and I would arrive just in time to console her.

I felt like the worst grandson *ever* for even considering such a dastardly deed, but there didn't seem to be any other reasonable option.

The next challenge would be to find a veterinarian who not only made house calls, but who would be willing to do it. I checked with my grandmother's lawyer and he confirmed that, as the holder of my grandmother's power of attorney and personal directive, it was my decision to make.

I called several veterinary clinics and explained the situation. Most of them told me that they didn't do house calls, or that they were booked solid leading up to the Christmas holidays. A couple of them suggested offhand that what I was planning wasn't a very charitable thing to be doing just before the holidays.

Eventually, I found a vet on Edmonton's east side who spoke with a thick Russian accent. I can't recall our exact conversation, but I think it went something like this:

"I have a little problem that needs to go away," I told him.

"What you like I should do?" he asked.

"There's this dog, see, that needs to have a little accident. My grandmother's dog."

"No problem. I can make very good accident. Your grandma no suspect a thing."

"How much will it cost?"

"So, let me think. How about one million dollars?"

"One *million*? We're talking about a dog. A yappy one at that!"

"OK. For you I make good price. How about *fifty* dollars?"

"That's more like it."

Actually, I made that conversation up. It didn't actually happen that way.

Basically, I explained the situation to the vet and he confirmed that he could do what I needed him to do. But before he would commit to doing it, he wanted to speak to my grandmother's lawyer. I gave him the lawyer's phone number and faxed him a copy of her power of attorney. With that out of the way, I bought two airplane tickets—one for me and one for my grandmother—and arranged for the "mob hit" to happen the day before we were to fly back to Ontario. My grandma hadn't been to Ontario for many years, since Poopsie didn't travel well. I figured that being with family at Christmastime would help to ease the pain of losing Poopsie.

On the morning Dr. Doom was to pay his visit, I got an urgent phone call from my grandma's best friend, Elsie. I had told Elsie what I was planning to do. As I wouldn't be able to make it to Edmonton until later in the day, I wanted her to be aware of the situation in case my grandma needed some companionship right after the incident.

"Your grandmother called me this morning. She told me that her sister Mary passed on last night," Elsie said.

"Oh, no," I said. This was unfortunate news, but at the same time I knew that Mary was almost ninety and had been bedridden for some time. It wasn't entirely unexpected.

"Your grandma told me that she's not going down for lunch today."

The penny dropped. "Oh … no!"

After I had hung up with Elsie, I called my grandma. A sad voice answered the phone.

"Hi Grandma. It's me, Matt."

"Mary passed on last night," she said. She had obviously been crying.

"I'm so sorry to hear that," I replied. "I know how much you loved her."

"She was kind of a mean sister," said my grandma.

"Well, yes, I've heard you mention that before." Apparently she and Mary didn't always see eye to eye on things. And Mary used to tease her mercilessly.

"I'm not going down for lunch today."

"Really?" I said. "You should think about it. You'd probably feel better if you ate something and talked to your friends."

"I've got Poopsie here to make me feel better." I could hear Poopsie yapping in the background, and my heart sank.

How could I go through with this now?

We talked for another few minutes, and I tried to leave her with some comforting words. After hanging up I frantically dialed the number for the veterinarian, hoping to catch him before he left his clinic. There was no answer.

I called the care home office and got John on the line. I explained the situation to him, and asked him what he thought we should do.

Tension crackled over the telephone. It wasn't so much what he said, but how he said it, that made it abundantly clear I had already called in my last favor. "That dog has to go," he said. "He can't stay here any longer."

"Alright, alright," I said. "I'm calling in sick at my job and driving up to Edmonton right now. When the vet comes, would you please ask him if he can come back at dinnertime?" I knew it was a long shot, but I didn't know what else to do.

John reluctantly agreed.

On the drive up to Edmonton, I had the distinct sense that God was trying to send me a message. Was it possible that plotting to knock off my grandmother's dog was inappropriate by His standards?

When I arrived in Edmonton, John told me that the vet couldn't make it back that evening, but that he was going to come back the following day at lunchtime.

"But I'm supposed to fly out with my grandma tomorrow morning," I said. "She'll never get on the airplane if Poopsie is still alive."

John shrugged. "I don't know what to tell you. That's the best I can do. We'll have a mutiny here if we wait any longer."

I nodded and thanked him. My insides felt like they were on fire.

I took Grandma out for dinner that night—to McDonald's. She had always loved McDonald's hamburgers. Then we went to the West Edmonton Mall to walk around for a while: I bought her some ice cream, and we wandered past the pet store to look at budgies and hamsters.

When we got back to the care home, we could hear Poopsie yapping from the far end of the hall as soon as we stepped off the elevator. I could see Mrs. Jones standing in the doorway of her apartment as we approached, a harrowed look on her face. I smiled at her. She did not smile back.

"You know, she's not a very nice woman," said my grandma after we were inside her apartment. "She never smiles."

I didn't sleep very well that night, and the next morning I flew to Ontario. Despite Elsie's assurances that she and her husband would keep an eye on Grandma over the holidays, I worried how she would react to losing her dog.

When my mother picked me up at the Toronto airport, she confirmed that the hit had been successful. Poopsie had been found in his doggie bed, curled up as if he was asleep.

What I would find out later, from John, is that my grandmother had been invited out for lunch that day by my Uncle Duncan and Aunt Doreen, who just happened to be in town from northern Alberta. They knew nothing about "the plot," so John had looked on with great trepidation as they waved at him on their way past the office and accompanied my grandmother up to her apartment.

About a half hour later my Uncle Duncan came down to the office. "Excuse me," he said to John. "Clara's little dog seems to be dead."

"Oh dear," said John. "How unfortunate. Is there anything we can do?"

"Would you happen to have a box?" asked Duncan. "We'd like to take the dog to Clara's vet so that we can have an autopsy done."

"Really? Why would you want to do that?"

"To find out the cause of death, of course."

John couldn't believe what he was hearing. He had reluctantly pulled Duncan into his office, shut the door, and confessed the entire story. Thankfully, my Uncle Duncan understood, though he did tell John that he wouldn't mention it to my Aunt Doreen. "She probably wouldn't understand," he said.

On Christmas Day I called my grandma on the phone, and was surprised that she sounded so chipper. "Grandma, you sound really happy," I said. "I know it's not easy when you lose a good friend like Poopsie."

"He was getting old," she said, her voice momentarily cracking.

"Yes, he was. I'm sure he's running around in doggie heaven as we speak."

She brightened. "I'm sure he is," she said. "By the way, Doreen called me today and said that she's going to buy me another dog."

Doreen never did buy Matt's grandmother another dog. He made sure of that. A couple of weeks later, Matt also learned that reports of his grandma's sister Mary's demise had been greatly exaggerated. She was still very much alive. He can only conclude that his grandmother dreamed about the incident. After a long decade, he's finally come to terms with ordering a mob hit on Poopsie. Sort of.

Here's Kitty!

How much trouble could one little cat be?

By Greg Simison

The cat's here. My son, who will soon be moving back in with "dear old dad" after a year of living with "dear old mom," brought it along with the first carload of stuff last weekend. The last time I saw this thing (the cat, not my son) was about a year ago in Toronto and it was just emerging from the kitten stage. Since then it has just kept emerging and emerging and emerging, rapidly racing up the evolutionary ladder to become some giant specimen of feline life.

I'll make it clear from the start that I like cats, though I tend to like them more when they live elsewhere. When my kids were small we had as many as seven cats sharing the house with us, but as I aged I found I had less and less patience for dealing with them. You can only spend so many years getting up in the mornings and stepping on liquid hair balls on your way to the bathroom before it starts to wear you down. Not to mention the cost of hiring gravel trucks to deliver your weekly supply of kitty litter and haul away the reeking mounds of used stuff.

Over the years a combination of fast cars and slow cats reduced their population to a manageable level (the advantage of living on a busy street). Those that survived the crossing eventually succumbed to old age or wandered off in search of greener litter boxes. The last surviving cats opted to move out with my daughter rather than stay and deal with the evil gleam in my eye (recall Jack Nicholson's mad expression in *The Shining* as he hunted down his family).

After an enjoyable year without cats, I reluctantly agreed to let my son bring his along, with the understanding that he would be completely responsible for its care and upkeep. Evidence of how stupid I am.

"Oh, come on," my ex-wife said when I expressed reservations about taking the cat. "How much trouble will one little kitty be? He's so gentle and well behaved. You'll love him."

I believed her. Yet more evidence of my stupidity.

I knew something was wrong when I saw the smile on her face as she followed my son into the apartment. While he struggled to drag the carrying-cage —which suspiciously resembled a heavily reinforced shark cage—into the living room, her smile grew even broader. It's difficult to describe what came out when he finally bent down to open the door and release "kitty" into his new home. It was like watching a half-starved wolverine, or the Tasmanian Devil from the Bugs Bunny Show, come to life before my eyes. A blur exploded from the cage and raced down the hallway toward my bedroom, its razor-sharp claws removing wide strips of wallpaper along the way.

"Your cat has arrived," my grinning ex-wife announced. Regardless of how amicable our divorce, no opportunity for revenge is ever passed up.

On Monday she left with my son to drive back home, leaving the cat and me to work out some sort of living arrangement until my son returned at the end of the school year. I knew it would be a difficult adjustment for both of us since they took the cat's best friend and playmate with them, a black lab/pit bull cross. The cat had spent its life play fighting with this monster and rumor has it the dog hasn't won a single match; which is understandable when you consider how all that scar tissue restricts its flexibility. I noted that the dog didn't shed a single tear as it climbed into the car and attempted to wave goodbye with its right front stump. I suspected that I would be in a difficult situation when it came to disciplining the kitty from hell, and that situation wasn't long in coming.

I was foolish enough the next afternoon to attempt to punish the cat for some slight misdemeanor: tearing off the fridge door in order to reach my milk stash. I rolled up a newspaper and approached the creature, milk still dripping from its gaping maw, and swung at its ugly head. A retaliatory swipe of its paw reduced the rolled paper to confetti. I spent the next hour locked in the bathroom until the cat exhausted itself trying to claw through the inch-thick door.

By Wednesday a shaky truce was established and we did our best to stay out of one another's way. This arrangement worked well during the day, but new conflicts arose at night when it decided it couldn't live without my company. Rather than let it pace outside my closed bedroom door screeching its head off, and filling every watchdog in the neighborhood with terror, I surrendered and let it curl up on the end of my bed. It was like sleeping with an obese cougar. I woke every morning and with trepidation counted all my limbs, half-expecting to look over and see the thing in the corner chewing on one of my legs.

It was at that point I decided the situation called for drastic action. I talked my daughter's boyfriend into taking the cat for a long one-way drive. The fifty bucks I offered helped. With the assistance of four neighbors we managed to throw a blanket over the struggling monster and tossed it into the trunk of the car, the damage limited to one torn-off fender and a missing thumb. As he drove off, I felt a twinge of guilt for about a millisecond.

Three hours later the cat returned. Driving the car.

At that point I gave up. I know when I'm licked. I can only hope the diet of prime rib and clotted cream the cat insists on will quickly lead to heart failure.

On the bright side, the boyfriend has yet to find his way back.

Greg Simison is a writer living in Moose Jaw, Saskatchewan. His fifth book, Miscellaneous Wreckage, *was released by Thistledown Press in 2014. The cat from hell was left behind by his son, and passed away shortly thereafter without ever divulging the whereabouts of the boyfriend's body.*

The Mynahs of Mazerolle

They were the talk of the town.

By Sylvia Shawcross

They were purchased in Germany in 1962 from a loud and foul-smelling pet store on the outskirts of Hemer, where my father had been posted by the Canadian military. Mahoop, Mahatt, and Gandhi were fat little bundles of feathers that had not yet learned to fly or to talk, as Mynah birds are wont to do when in the company of people. When they weren't in our living room splashing about in the water of a red-rimmed mixing bowl that we had turned into a birdbath, they lived in separate cages.

Baths were often necessary because they were messy birds. When they sat on your fingers they would often squat and poop. And everything you fed them—they particularly liked grapes—the birds would fling and smash against their perches. Even when they were drinking water in their cages they somehow managed to spray it everywhere. Little drops would inevitably land on top of my head because they were always up high and I was the smallest in the family. When I complained, my father—because he fancied himself a pun artist—would say with a smile, "It's your rain of terror." I eventually accepted that it sometimes rained inside the house just for me.

When we returned to Canada we were initially refused permission to board the great ship that would carry us home because records showed there should have been six children: Anne, Charles, Sylvia, Mahoop, Mahatt and Gandhi. They counted us several times. "One. Two. Three," they said, both officiously and suspiciously. I remember this because I myself was just learning how to count and I felt quite sad that persons so big were still unable to count to four.

It took a frantic few hours to convince officials that one of my parents had filled in a form with six children somewhere along the line in a small act of anti-bureaucratic rebellion. I suspect it was my mother because of that Cape Breton heritage of hers, but it could just as easily have been my father, who spent our entire grade school existence writing witty comments on our school report cards. If you gave my father a form and a pen, all societal norms broke down. He would fill in the little boxed areas and then add attachments. I think my father wanted to start a revolution one day, but he never did get that far because he always ended up as a bureaucrat on the wrong side of all potential social unrest. When he worked managing the construction of the King's Landing Historical Settlement, he stood in front of a horde of angry men threatening to strike because the pork chops they were being fed tasted terrible. He had to break the news that they were actually eating lamb, and the only revolution he was ever to partake in quickly disintegrated into chagrin. Yes, it was probably my father who had filled in those forms.

Once the officials had established what types of birds we had—and we had signed all the necessary papers to export the birds—we were finally ready to board the ship. That was when I piped up and asked, with the innocence of a typical four-year-old, about the turtles in my brother's pockets. The officials were quiet for what seemed a very long time. I remember them looking at me, shaking their heads, and then simply waving us on board the ship. From there we made our way across the shimmering sea to Halifax, and then on to a farmhouse in Mazerolle Settlement, near Fredericton, New Brunswick.

Mahoop, Mahatt, and Gandhi did not settle in quite so easily. Every morning in the summer, two of us would haul their cage out to the porch so they could sit in the sun. Gandhi, sleek and shiny, became a marvel of imitation with a crystal-clear vocabulary of well over one thousand words. She lived most of her twenty-eight years with Mahatt, who was flat-headed and somewhat stupid. Mahoop partitioned himself at the other end of the cage because Gandhi had taken a disliking to him. Whenever they were together they would disappear into a swirl of fighting feathers. Mahoop never won a match, but he nevertheless outlived Gandhi by at least five years.

It was Mahatt who became a problem.

My parents initially put the birdcage in the hallway outside their master bedroom, but Mahatt began to imitate my father's snoring. Except that Mynah birds seemingly amplify the sound tenfold. My mother said she could not handle my father's snoring night *and* day, so the birds were moved to the other end of the hallway, just outside the bathroom. So Mahatt began to *swoosh* like the toilet instead. My father, being British, found the sounds of any bathroom activity to be deeply impolite, so the birds were moved yet again to the front entry by the telephone.

Our problems continued. Gandhi began imitating the British accent of my mother's friend Mrs. Clark. "Hello!" Gandhi would screech in the most insulting parody of a British accent, which to our surprise offended Mrs. Clark even though the perpetrator was a bird. And so the cage went on top of the fridge, where Mahatt happily gurgled like the freezer and whistled like the kettle, making it difficult to know if tea was actually on or not. And every time he imitated the kettle, Gandhi would screech, "Put the kettle on! Put the kettle on!" We must have had tea twelve times a day back then, until my parents got so sick of it that they placed the birdcage in our family room under Amos the stuffed moose, which is where I suspect the birds had intended to be all the time.

When new people came to visit we would hide the birds in another room, but there was always a cacophony of odd voices and whistles that found their way downstairs. If they were in a teasing kind of mood, my parents would tell the guests that they had another child who was "a bit odd," until they could no longer carry on the charade. My mother usually gave it away first because she never developed a poker face.

We often brought the birds with us when we went to town. I spent a large percentage of my childhood in a variety of parking lots with the rear hatch of our Volkswagen van open. When they first heard the birds, people would approach us cautiously at first, but would quickly warm to the performers. I made sure that people removed their hats because Gandhi wouldn't talk if they had them on; I also informed people not to put their fingers near the birds because Mahoop would surely bite.

Gandhi would often greet onlookers with the one-liner: "Go away, you bother me." Some people would actually walk away, a sad look on their faces, and I would have to chase after them to apologize. At other times visitors would ask questions, and I would always let Gandhi answer first.

"How should *I* know?" she'd usually screech.

My mother taught them the most curious things: "Have a tea," or "Who won the ballgame?" When I became a teenager I spent a great deal of time cringing in the van, hiding if I could, because Mahoop knew how to wolf-whistle. Recall that Mynah birds can increase the sound tenfold.

We took the birds to Fredericton's Great Centennial Exhibition in 1967 for a showing, and to our chagrin they said nothing. Not a whistle. Not a grunt. Not a gurgle or a single word. For three agonizing days we tried to coax something—*anything*—out of them. But it was all to no avail. My mother claimed it was because they resented the man with the chicken incubator in the booth next to us. Personally, I believe it was Gandhi's fault. She was a spiteful little bird who had her own way of fun.

Case in point: we didn't even know Gandhi was a "she" until 1971, when she ruined our watching of the Apollo mission by laying an egg. "What's up, doc?" she said. We spent the entire Apollo mission looking for an incubator for eggs that never hatched.

The Mynahs later traveled with us across the country on our way to Meadow Lake, Saskatchewan. All along the route—in campgrounds and in parking lots—the rear hatch of our van would open so that the birds could get a little fresh air and sunshine.

Gandhi would sing "Hello," while Mahoop wolf-whistled and Mahatt gurgled like a toilet. Small clusters of people would gather in amazement. It was just the way it was.

Those days are gone, of course, but sometimes I like to think there are those in Canada who smile when they remember the Mynahs of Mazerolle.

Sylvia Shawcross lives in the forested hills of Chelsea, Quebec, but her heart belongs to the Maritimes. She writes a humor column for The West Quebec Post, *and in 2011 she won the award for Best Columnist in Quebec by the Quebec Community Newspaper Association. She is also the author of two books:* Never Mind All That *and* The Get-Over-Yourself Self-Help Book. *In the words of Farley Mowat, she is "that rarity of our times, an honest-to-god satirist." As such, Shawcross loves to rail against the insanity of our world in her unique curmudgeonly style.*

Kima

The trials and tribulations of a first-time mother in Africa.

By Sharon Fitzsimmons

We were in our mid-twenties, newly married, and on the trip of our lives. It was 1972, and my husband Doug and I had spent two years scrimping and saving so we could quit our jobs and embark on a four-month overland journey from London, England to Nairobi, Kenya. We traveled in Land Rovers and slept in canvas tents. Although the trip was not easy or fun, it was always memorable.

Despite encountering exotic sights and sounds almost every day, we weren't prepared for the day we would first meet Kima. When I close my eyes, I can still see the long tuft of black hair that stuck straight up into a peak, the way her big black eyes sparkled when she laughed, and how her long slender tail curled up and over her back, almost touching her head. You see, Kima was not just any baby girl; she was a baby monkey, and during our time together she would steal our hearts.

We first laid eyes on Kima as we were driving along a road in Zaire (now the Congo). As we drove by—eight foreigners squished into a Land Rover—the natives held her up to show that she was for sale. At the time, Kima couldn't have been more than a few weeks old, and was so small that she could sit comfortably inside a man's palm. The mother monkey would have stood about a meter tall, so she had already been killed for her meat. Fortunately, Kima's tiny body had probably saved her from a similar fate.

Doug stopped the vehicle so we could get a better look. As soon as I held her and felt how frail she was, I couldn't let her go; she would surely have been thrown to the dogs. Doug pragmatically realized that he would have a very unhappy wife and traveling companion if he refused to take the monkey, so he offered the princely sum of two dollars for her. Apparently pleased with our deal, the local natives quickly handed her over. And that's how we came to be the proud owners—or should I say first-time adoptive parents—of a completely dependent newborn monkey. We called her Kima, short for *Mukaku-kima*, which means "monkey" in Swahili. We later found out that Kima was a rare breed called Black Mangabey.

If only we'd known what we were getting ourselves into.

It didn't take long to realize that looking after little Kima was a huge responsibility. Any woman who has experienced the emotional and physical rollercoaster of looking after a newborn baby will attest to that. Our most immediate concern was how to feed her. She was young enough to still be nursing, and with her mother gone, she looked a bit malnourished. We bought some canned condensed milk from the market and discovered that if we put some on our fingers, she would lick it off. Later, mashed bananas appeased her growing appetite.

As with any baby, there were round-the-clock feedings, diaper changes, and cuddling time. But Kima was even more dependent. As she would have done with her natural mother, Kima spent every moment of the next four months attached to either my body or Doug's. Even those few seconds of air time when she was being transferred from one to the other would cause poor Kima to panic, scream, and pee all over us. I even had to devise a way to dress in stages, relocating Kima to different parts of my body as the dressing progressed. As tiring as it was to look after such a dependent young animal, I relished my bond with Kima, and was somewhat saddened when she eventually grew old enough to start exploring the world more independently.

By the time we arrived in Kenya several weeks later, Kima was growing quickly and had all her hair, but she was still very clingy. Like any baby, she spent her time sleeping, eating, peeing, and making funny expressions. You couldn't help but laugh just looking at her, with a pink bow in her four-inch tuft of head hair, and a diaper with a hole cut out for her tail. Her many human qualities made it easy to forget that she was an animal. She would wake up in the morning, stretch her arms and yawn. Mind you, she also scratched her tummy and her crotch, but teaching her proper manners was too daunting a task.

The group safari ended in Nairobi, where Doug and I spent a tearful day saying goodbye to all our new friends. At the same time, we knew that we had to make a big decision for ourselves: should we return home to Canada or continue traveling on our own through Africa?

Thirty years ago, Africa was not as well-traveled by foreigners as it is today. The inherent dangers, combined with money shortages, made it look like Canada would be the best choice. But just when we were resigned to returning home, we struck a windfall. Doug was offered a lecturer's position in the Faculty of Computer Science at the University of Johannesburg. We were ecstatic to prolong our trip, and spent a month living in a run-down hotel in Nairobi, waiting for Doug's papers for teaching in South Africa to be approved.

During this time, Kima started to explore. At first, she only dared to venture a few steps from us, and would always run back at the first hint of trouble. I often tucked her into my suspiciously oversized purse at the movies or at fancy restaurants. At one particularly upscale restaurant, I transferred her from my purse to my lap. Our dinner table rule was that she couldn't eat from our plates but she was allowed to have any scraps we put beside our plates. Over the course of dinner, I glanced at the next table and saw our neighboring diner's eyes open wide in astonishment. All he could see was a hairy black hand reaching up from under my napkin to grope around my plate until it found whatever piece of fruit I had left there. To his surprise, the hand grabbed the fruit and disappeared, only to reappear moments later to grope for the next piece. I felt an explanation was necessary, so I discreetly revealed Kima on my lap. Her pitch-black face and wide black eyes, accented by three ridiculously long whiskers poking straight up above each eye, won him over. The man smiled and went back to his dinner.

We experienced a lot of firsts with Kima. In fact, we still have the old super-eight home videos of Kima's first tree. Well, it wasn't a tree so much as a small sapling about a meter high. But for Kima, it was her first major challenge, since she was probably only about eight inches tall at the time. This "tree" was so wiry that Kima's full four pounds, when perched at the very top of the tree, were enough to bend it all the way to the ground, where she could safely jump off. Once she mastered this tree-climbing exercise, it became her favorite game.

After a month in Nairobi, Doug's papers came through, so we flew to Johannesburg, South Africa. The airline's rules dictated that animals had to be in the cargo area of the plane, but that would have been absolutely traumatic for Kima, who had never been more than a meter away from us. So we smuggled her onto the plane. First we drugged her with a mild tranquilizer that we got from a sympathetic veterinarian at the university of Nairobi. We waited until the last minute to board, hid her inside Doug's jean jacket, and made our way to customs.

Unfortunately, we had overstayed our Kenyan visas and the customs clerk spent several minutes chewing us out. Later, we realized he was getting us to pay him, but being the naïve Canadians we are, we didn't understand. Meanwhile, we were sweating. Kima was inside Doug's jacket, but her tail was hanging below it, advertising her presence. Luckily, the clerk couldn't see anything below the counter, so he remained oblivious to our traveling companion.

For many long minutes we stood at that counter until one of the flight attendants rushed up to us and asked if we were Doug and Sharon Fitzsimmons. We were the last passengers to board the plane and they were holding it for us. With that, Doug turned to the customs guard and said, "Sorry, but we have to go." We took off running toward the plane, grinning the whole way.

Once the plane was in the air, we felt that we were safe; Kima came out of hiding and all the flight attendants came over to take a closer look. She was still a bit groggy, but was willing to smile and be cute. It was only after landing in Johannesburg that the pilot came up to us and voiced his displeasure. He was angry that we had smuggled her onto his plane. He was a loud, arrogant man who kept insisting that he would have killed Kima if he had known she was on board. The idea of anyone hurting poor Kima made me break into sobs, but apparently that's what he had set out to do, since he left us alone after I started crying.

South Africa had a one-month quarantine requirement for out-of-country monkeys, so Kima was taken from us and put into quarantine. This was to be our most significant separation yet, and I worried terribly how Kima would fare. As it turned out, I should have been worried about how I would fare, since I seemed to take our separation harder than Kima did. Luckily, the facilities were clean and new. Kima even had a cage to herself. It was only a meter wide, but about three meters high and three meters long— more than enough room for her to jump around in. The workers were very kind and allowed me to visit every day, which was good for both of us. Finally, after about two weeks, the workers cut us some slack and let us take her home early. Or maybe they were just sick of seeing my face pressed against the window every morning, begging to be let inside.

Home for us was an apartment over some stores in a run-down area of Johannesburg, within walking distance of the University of Witwatersrand. Kima had the run of our apartment and we felt like a family again. Only once did we leave the apartment without her, and we had to hire a babysitter to make sure the house would still be intact by the time we came home. The rest of the time, Kima was our constant companion while we explored our new city, which meant we were always surrounded by curious people.

Even though South Africa has a lot of wild monkeys, it is illegal to own a monkey unless it is from another country. She was adorable, and like any proud first-time mother, I loved all the attention my baby received. By now she didn't want to be in my purse and would instead sit on Doug's shoulders and hang on to his hair. Kima was becoming more independent, and since we had a steady paycheck from Doug's job, so were we. We decided to use the last of our funds to purchase a Volkswagen Beetle, outfitted for life on the road.

We spent many days in that car, visiting everywhere that lay within a few days' driving distance. Doug's teaching schedule permitted four-day weekends and we made the most of them. Kima took great pleasure in sitting on the top of the back seat, enjoying the view. Every once in a while she got lonely back there and would join us in the front seat. Instead of walking down the seat, however, Kima did what monkeys do—she grabbed a hunk of Doug's hair and swung herself forward. There was never any warning when this might happen, and it added a new dimension of challenge to driving, for Doug would have to keep us on the road while Kima used his hair as a vine.

To avoid this, we tried to come up with ways to keep her occupied. As with every toddler, we found that distracting her with food worked quite well. She especially liked grapes, but she was fussy and wouldn't eat the skins. She didn't mind peeling them herself, but then she would leave the dried-up skins all over the car. To protect our car, I relented and peeled all the grapes before we left home.

Doug had other struggles with Kima. When we weren't traveling, Kima enjoyed sitting on Doug's chest or shoulders, picking through his hair to look for bits of salt or bugs. At fairly regular intervals, certain that she had spotted some intruding insect, Kima would grab a fistful of Doug's hair, yank it out by the roots, and hold it up to her face so close that she would go cross-eyed staring at it. Inevitably, she would realize that nothing was there, shake the recently uprooted hair onto the floor, and continue searching. This was certainly a primary cause of Doug's premature balding.

To protect our apartment, I also toilet trained Kima. About every two hours, I would perch her on the toilet seat and command in a singsong voice, "Go pee-pee, Kima. Go pee-pee." This was usually followed by the telltale noises of a good monkey following orders. I have no doubt Kima would have been fully toilet trained, except she couldn't lift her tail out of the toilet water. African monkeys, as opposed to American monkeys, have no control over their tails. So my role became that of tail-holder during Kima's bathroom visits. What a mother doesn't do for her baby!

By then, Kima was an expert climber, and her climbing toys had extended from that first scrawny tree to include Doug and myself, the furniture, and best of all, the family room drapes. One of Kima's favorite games was to dash up the drapes, stand poised on the curtain rod, and then leap off with four legs spread wide. She always seemed visibly thrilled at the ferocious CRASH! she made when she landed on newspapers that were usually strewn on the couch.

The game worked fine until "Grandma" came for a visit.

Doug's mom flew from Windsor, Ontario to Johannesburg for a week-long visit. Being a young wife, I was very aware that she seemed to regard me as the woman who had caused Doug to lose his mind, quit his job, and spend years traveling in Africa. Grandma was a very conservative, hard-working woman. Until this visit, her most distant trip had been to move from her prairie homestead in Saskatchewan to Ontario, and she made it clear that she did not approve of the frivolous expenditures Doug and I were making on this trip.

In addition, she was highly suspicious about keeping a wild monkey in the apartment. I was determined to spend the week proving that I was a good wife, and that traveling to Africa wasn't nearly as scary as Grandma assumed. So it was much to my chagrin that I found Grandma napping on the couch one afternoon with the newspaper lightly folded across her chest.

I immediately took stock of the situation, scanning the room to find Kima. Sure enough, she was exactly where I'd hoped she wouldn't be—hanging off the drapes. Kima and I locked eyes, and by the excited gleam on her face, I knew exactly what she had in mind. I lunged for Kima, but she was too quick, playfully dodging my attempt to stop the inevitable. There she sat on the curtain rod, carefully analyzing the best angle from which to leap. I whispered urgently to Kima, explaining why she couldn't— really shouldn't—jump on Grandma. All the while, Kima stood with her legs outstretched and her head angled forward and down like a high-diver, preparing for her most challenging dive yet.

Finally, I decided to get a chair so I could reach Kima. As soon as I turned my back, of course, Kima grabbed the opportunity and made like a flying squirrel. She propelled herself off the drapes with all the power her tiny body could muster. She dropped through the air with her little hands flailing, only to land with a satisfying CRASH! squarely on the newspapers laid across my soundly sleeping mother-in-law. Did I say soundly sleeping? Never before had one of Kima's jumps produced a noise quite like the one that erupted from Grandma as she woke to find a writhing ball of monkey scrambling across her. Poor Grandma. It took a few minutes to calm her down, and I doubt she slept much during the rest of her visit. So much for making a good impression!

Kima was almost a year old by the time Doug's contract at the university was complete, and we were again faced with a tough decision. Now that we had replenished our bank account, we decided to head back home to Toronto via South America. But how could we bring Kima along? I spent many hours contacting consulates and permit offices, trying to find a way to keep Kima with us. But most countries didn't allow monkeys, and if caught, she would either be killed or put in quarantine for at least six months.

Given the dismal reports of conditions in human jails in those countries, I didn't event want to consider what the animal quarantines would be like. The chances of getting caught were too great. With our hearts broken, the only option was to find her a new home.

The zoo didn't want her because they knew the other monkeys would reject and probably kill her. It wasn't an option to set Kima free, either. Not only had she been coddled and spoiled for all her young life, but Kima was a North African monkey. She was completely unprepared for the conditions and predators of South Africa.

Eventually, we heard about a family who lived on a farm near Pretoria, just north of Johannesburg. This family was unique because they kept zoo animals instead of farm animals. After hearing our story, they agreed to meet Kima. It didn't take long for them to fall in love with her the same way Doug and I had a year earlier. She was bigger and bolder now, but loved to be cuddled by anyone who was willing to give her attention. Not surprisingly, they were thrilled to adopt Kima.

Although I was grateful to have found a loving home for her, I was not yet satisfied. There was no way I could give up my baby without doing a thorough background check on the couple who were taking her in. On more than one occasion, Kima and I would pop in unexpectedly, half-hoping to catch them in the act of some evildoing. On one late-night espionage mission, I cautiously tiptoed up to their family room window to peer in and see how they were treating their animals. After several minutes of watching and listening, I tiptoed away again, smiling sheepishly, finally convinced that the family really was as loving as they proclaimed. The mom had been tenderly knitting a sweater for Kima, whose native Zaire was much more tropical than the high country of South Africa.

Despite the loving family we gave her to, I can still feel the pain of giving her up. It was a deep wrench in my gut that, even after thirty-three years, I can feel as I remember her sweet little-girl ways. We brought her to the farm about a month before leaving for South America so we could be sure it was working out. Every few days I would make a surprise visit to see if they were treating her well. But it was obvious they loved her. She was loose on their farm during the day and slept in the house at night. Finally, I was satisfied she would get the attention and love she deserved.

You can perhaps imagine our anguish, then, the day the farm called with some sad news, a few days before Doug and I were to fly to South America. "I'm sorry Sharon, I have some bad news. Kima passed on during the night." There was a long pause on the other end of the phone. "We don't know why. She must have picked up some virus that she wasn't accustomed to fending off. We brought her to the zoo veterinarian this morning, but he couldn't do anything to help her. I'm so sorry."

We never saw Kima again.

Little Kima was with us for only a year, but we'll always love and cherish the memories we have of her. Would it have been better not to interfere in the first place? If we hadn't, she likely wouldn't have survived as long as she did. Of course, we don't know the answer. All we know is that she brought unimaginable love and joy into our lives. We like to think she remembers us as the parents every young monkey should have.

Doug and Sharon Fitzsimmons currently split their time between retirement communities in Guelph, Ontario, and The Villages, Florida. They have two children who are not only potty trained, but have earned Doctorate degrees.

Doggone Nuisance

How an unwanted pooch earned his keep.

By Stuart Reininger

A blast of cold air slapped me across the face as I cracked open the companionway hatch. On deck, a layer of snow covered the cockpit seats, even as stalactites of ice rimmed the wheel. My eyes moved to the dock and I saw that *he* was there again.

The mutt—looking as woebegone as I felt—was sitting on the pier. As soon as he spotted me he began shivering.

"Great act," I muttered as I tossed him a piece of bread.

The dog had shown up at the yard a week earlier. I had thrown him some scraps and the next morning he was camped at my doorstep. At least he had a good reason for being there—he was a homeless mutt looking for a handout. Me? I should've been basking in the Florida sun. But, no. I was hunkered down for the winter in a godforsaken New Jersey marina, a poster child for the maxim that "Greed cometh before the fall."

In my case, greed came before the winter. As a yacht delivery captain, my lucrative season was the fall. My primary job was to take boats from the northeastern coast of the U.S. to Florida, the Bahamas, and the Caribbean. I always made as many trips as possible before winter arrived, then sailed south on my own boat. That year, anxious for the buck, I squeezed in an extra late-season delivery. When I rushed back to Jersey to grab my boat and get out of Dodge, a string of vicious storms roared in. That was it. I wasn't going anywhere. I gritted my teeth, dug out my old Aladdin blue flame kerosene heater, and hunkered down for the next few months.

One morning I opened the hatch to the roar of a blizzard. The outline of the dock was almost indistinguishable from the drifts. And there was that doggone mutt again; this time, he looked more like a shivering mound of snow than a warm-blooded creature. He gazed at me longingly. Oh, for cryin' out loud!

"Alright, why don't you come..." *Whoosh!* Before I could finish the sentence, a blur of wet snow-covered dog barreled past me.

By the time I turned around, the mutt was stretched out on my bunk.

"Not there, you, you..." I gestured towards the other bunk. "That's where you'll sleep." He climbed down docilely.

"Wait. Let me get a towel."

He stopped. He gave me a questioning look, and then stood still as I dried him off. He might be a doggone mutt, but at least he wasn't stupid.

"Wow, what a great dog. Where did you find him, Dad?" My daughter, Karin, had come by to commiserate with me on my lousy luck.

"His name is Doggone Mutt," I growled. "And he's only here until I can figure out how to get rid of him."

"Let's call him Pepper," she said as she scratched him behind the ear.

"He's nothing like Pepper," I retorted. Pepper was our long-departed German shorthaired pointer—a beautiful purebred. The closest resemblance the hapless Doggone had to Pepper was a few livered spots amongst a ragged assortment of dirty brown splotches and blemishes. "I will not tarnish Pepper's memory in such a way."

As much as I wanted to get rid of Doggone, a long and lonely winter made it unlikely. And he was, I had to admit, a friendly dog.

Doggone and I shared our meals and discussed concerns about the world and life. His were straightforward concerns, mainly involving food and the elimination of waste. Mine were somewhat more complicated, having to do with the boat and my place in the overall scheme of things. I verbalized my concerns while Doggone listened patiently.

It was there in that forsaken boatyard in New Jersey that I renewed my faith in God—oops, I'm a bit dyslexic—I mean Dog. Or possibly a bit of both.

The night of my redemption began with a particularly heavy snowfall. As was my habit, I lowered the flame of the Aladdin heater and cracked the companionway hatch to allow for ventilation. Doggone and I then took to our respective bunks.

I awoke several hours later gasping for air. I sat up, but immediately collapsed as my head began to throb. Not only that; there was an inexplicably sharp pain in my ankle. I tried to ignore it. My headache receded and I began to drift off again. But the pain in my ankle wouldn't let me sleep—it was unbearable.

I forced myself up onto an elbow. The throbbing in my head renewed, now accompanied by a wave of nausea. I just wanted the pain to go away. I looked down and saw that Doggone was sprawled at an unnatural angle—his body on the floor, his head resting on my feet. In the flickering yellow light I saw that he had sunk his teeth into my ankle! There was blood on the floor, blood on his snout, blood all over the bunk. I reached over and grabbed him by the scruff of the neck. He was like a rag doll. I pushed him away and his head thumped against the floor. Was he dead?

I still hadn't understood what was happening—until I realized that I couldn't breathe. That's when I realized that the cabin was infused with a yellowish haze. The flickering low flame of the bulkhead-mounted kerosene lamp—combined with the blue flame of the Aladdin—was creating a dance of grotesque shadows on the walls.

A wave of panic washed over me. I rolled out of the bunk, stumbled over Doggone's body, and threw myself against the hatch. It burst open and cold air rushed in. I was too weak to even climb outside. I buried my face in the snow beside the hatch, which had obviously sealed the airway. I didn't feel the cold. I was too busy reveling in being alive.

Doggone was sprawled below, lifeless. In his death he had saved my life. Sobbing and shivering, I tried to pull him outside, but I could only manage to drag him to the companionway sill. I collapsed next to him. Incredibly, in that cold and wet snow, I drifted off to sleep.

I was awakened by Doggone licking my face.

That night Doggone's bunk became his permanent home. Unfortunately, he was not much of a seafaring dog. He never caught on that boats *move*. Over the winter he was able to hop on and off my boat at will. Come spring, however, as we motored away for the first time, he poised himself aft preparing for a leap that was obviously impossible. He gazed frantically at the receding dock, then up at me, and then back at the dock. He couldn't figure it out. Consequently, every time we approached shore he would begin vibrating as soon as land hove into sight. When we were close enough—and sometimes not close enough—he would leap for *terra firma* with an Olympian jump.

I didn't have the heart to subject Doggone to a long voyage, so whenever the need arose, I left him with Karin—who had renamed him Pepper. And Pepper he stayed until he joined his namesake in doggie heaven seven years later.

Stuart Reininger is a writer and charter captain who lives aboard his sloop Tall Tales. *Shortly after Doggone's departure, Stuart was adopted by an itinerant cat that he named Looney Tunes. As cats tend to do, Looney Tunes investigated every inch of the boat ... except for Doggone's old bunk, which he persistently avoided.*

Turkey Teeth

A gobbler makes his getaway.

By Lori Feldberg

My father-in-law, Gus, was living proof that a man doesn't need teeth in order to enjoy a wide variety of food. He gummed his grub quite successfully for many years, devouring everything but nuts until the ripe old age of ninety-nine.

Of course, I was always curious as to why he chose not to wear false teeth, and I finally got up the courage to ask the family. My husband, Jim, was only too happy to relate the events leading up to the demise of his dad's dentures. My husband entertained us with the story while his father sat in attendance, right there in the long-term care room. Jim had an audience, all of whom laughed uproariously while Gus maintained a straight face and kept trying to deny the truth of it. His denial might have worked, except my husband wasn't the only family member that had witnessed the episode.

Gus's teeth had been giving him trouble for years. Though he had only a few left, they proved to be very painful. Chewing tobacco and candy were apparently the cause of all his troubles. While he had eventually given up the chewing tobacco, his sweet tooth prevailed despite near agony whenever sugar found its way into the copious cavities that riddled his teeth. He eventually could stand it no longer, and braved the dentist's chair to have them pulled.

False teeth in the 1940s were nothing like what we're used to today. The oversized dentures filled his mouth "like a set of horse teeth," or so Gus would grumble. Nevertheless, he was able to chew meat reasonably well after he got the knack of it. He ate everything he wanted to.

But his false teeth were uncomfortable. He considered them especially bothersome when he didn't have anything to chew on. Why should he wear them all the time? He was not a vain person, so he started taking them out when he wasn't using them to eat, usually stuffing them in his front shirt pocket.

One day while he was milking a cow, his precious teeth suffered a mishap. While he bent over to set up his milk stool, they slipped out of his pocket and onto the ground. That wouldn't have been disastrous except that in his efforts to save them, he promptly stepped on them himself! Needless to say, the dentures broke and he spared no breath in expressing his upset at losing that first pair of false teeth.

After his second pair of dentures dropped out of his pocket and into a pail of milk at another milking (we had to drink the milk anyway), he decided that he'd best put them someplace other than his front pocket. Of course, he completely ignored the suggestion that he keep them in his mouth! So he took to laying them on the stone curb of the barn wall, where they would rest safely until the milking was finished.

Their farm had an assortment of critters—as did most farms in those days. Horses were necessary to carry on the activities of farming; cows were needed for meat and milk; chickens provided eggs; and turkeys made excellent dining for humans on festive occasions. The token dog and farmyard cats wandered around as they pleased. It wasn't unusual for a variety of livestock to pass through the barn while Gus was milking, so their comings and goings were for the most part ignored.

However, one evening after Gus had carefully placed his teeth on the stone curb and began his milking routine, a couple of turkeys wandered into the barn. One of them took a speculative glance at the dentures, and then as quick as a flash, snatched them up in his beak. Had he been given the opportunity to learn that they were hard and not very tasty, the gobbler probably would have discarded them. But with a yelp of dismay, Gus lunged at the perpetrator.

The turkey forgot about his prize in that he simply held on tight and fled the scene with Gus chasing close behind. If you're tempted to think turkeys are not good runners, you are sadly mistaken, for he remained a good twenty feet in front of Gus.

The pair dashed madly about the yard, scattering flocks of squawking chickens and romping calves as they went. Several fences were in the chaseway, which put Gus at a significant disadvantage. All of his hollering probably didn't help either.

Of course, my husband's family came out to see what the commotion was all about. It was such a hilarious sight—watching poor Gus chase after a turkey that was making off with his dentures—that they all started laughing rather than helping him corner the bird.

At some point the turkey decided that he needed to catch his breath, so he dropped his prize in favor of open-beak running. But Gus continued to chase the turkey. And my husband's family was laughing so hard that they couldn't shout out to tell him he was chasing the turkey for nothing.

About the time that both of them stopped to gasp for air, my husband's mother wisely herded the family back into the farmhouse, where they put on straight faces and seriously contemplated the potato soup bubbling on the stove. Gus was known to have a rather short temper if the joke was on him, so when he came inside with the pail of milk, everyone made sure to keep a very straight face.

When I asked Gus if he remembered when all of that had happened, he quickly shook his head. But, as he turned away, I was sure I saw a barely discernable grin on one side of his mouth.

Lori Feldberg performed fiction editor duties for Horizon Magazine *for over ten years, occasionally contributing true stories to the mix. She draws on both her own farm life experiences as well as her husband's amazing and often amusing memories. Just when she thinks she's run out of true-life tales, someone reminds her of another; those involving farm animals are her favorites.*

Heidi and Me

The life and times of the world's naughtiest dog. And we do mean naughtiest.

By Alice Newton

Have you ever shared your life with a yellow lab? If so, then you know they're capable of stamping an indelible emotional paw print on your heart. In my opinion, these dogs are the most beautiful, lovable, demented, exasperating canines ever to walk on our fine planet. My lab, Heidi, was a perfect case-in-point.

I have always harbored a soft spot for dogs, especially those with big, brown, soulful eyes. Less than one week after my husband, Jack, and I had moved into a home on a rural acreage near Victoria, Canada, I added my name to the waiting list at the local SPCA with the hope of adopting a puppy. I was overjoyed to hear that one was available only a week later!

Jack was at work when I got the news, and his teenage son Rob was still in bed following an all-night Dungeons & Dragons session. I knew that I'd require assistance to bring the pooch home. What to do? Fortunately, I found a half-conscious teenager named Johnny—the son of longtime friends who had slept over the previous night—stumbling around in the hallway attempting to find a bathroom. Wondering what it would take to lure the kid out to my vehicle, I came up with the idea to leave a trail of cold pizza slices that led toward the garage. With a teen thus secured and snoring softly in the rear of my Toyota, I sped recklessly towards the pound.

When I locked gazes with that gorgeous lab, *she* adopted *me*!

There hadn't been enough time to purchase a collar or leash for the dog, but I assumed she'd cuddle on my assistant's lap and settle down quickly. Little did I know that my acquisition would immediately adopt an alpha-dog mentality and use her forty-pound weight to pin little Johnny to the floorboards of my car. She drowned him in kisses and beat him half to death with her frantically wagging tail.

Jack had promised to treat the kids to stock car races that evening. We regretted having to leave our new family member behind, but it was a pleasant summer evening for her to be outside. We borrowed a collar and a long, thick rope, which we used to secure Heidi to our patio picnic table. But when we returned home, both the dog *and* the rope were gone! Heidi, of course, wouldn't recognize her owner's voice yet, so it was pointless trying to call for her. I went to bed sobbing into my pillow about love found and so soon relinquished.

The following day our neighbor's son told us that he'd been camping in the backyard the previous night. As the kids were telling ghost stories to each other, a shadow circled their tent and an animal burst through the open flap. At first they were terrified because they thought it was a cougar. But they quickly realized it was a hungry but friendly dog with a length of frayed rope trailing from her neck. They locked her in their fenced tennis court, hoping they could find the owner. We were thrilled to get her back.

On my second day as a puppy parent, I went shopping for all of Heidi's anticipated needs: Hudson's Bay blankets, a baby mattress, toys, bones, a selection of premium dried and canned foods, and vitamins. The first time we left her in the garage all tucked into her luxury bed set, she ripped the blanket to shreds, tore the stuffing out of the mattress, and upended her water bowl in the middle of the mess.

Day three saw the dog we now referred to as "Heidi, the hound from hell" climbing up onto the workbench to reach some shelves on which I'd stored extra items. She was not attracted to the year's worth of fake bedroom slippers, nor the chewy bones. Oh, no. She was somehow compelled to satisfy her appetite by eating a large can of flea powder. I rushed her off to the veterinarian. He was a diminutive gentleman, and I estimated that he and the dog weighed about the same. When he heard the story he instructed me to pick Heidi up, place her on the table, and hold her still while he pumped her stomach. A half hour and a hundred dollars later, we were on our way.

We thought Heidi might prefer being an outdoor animal, but where could we contain her? We left her in an unused chicken coop surrounded by a high fence. She dug *under* the fence. We filled in the holes and piled rocks around the perimeter. She climbed *over* the fence. We built her a nice kennel with a cedar shake roof. She wrapped her chain around a large Douglas fir tree and almost choked to death when the chain became too short. We moved the kennel out of harm's way and re-attached the chain. She towed the kennel the entire length of our driveway and detached herself from it. She returned later, reeking to high heaven in the aftermath of what must have been numerous glorious rolls through fresh cow pies and meadow muffins.

A family friend once came to spend the weekend with us. Martha must have had a sweet tooth, as the contents of her suitcase included a two-pound bag of Reese's Peanut Butter Cups. She left her suitcase unzipped on her bed and Heidi's sensitive nose led her straight to the prize. Heidi wolfed down the entire contents—the bag, wrappers, and aluminum cups included. That dog should have been ill. But her only reaction to eating the stash was to run around the yard crapping little ashtrays for the next two days.

Heidi had a ravenous appetite for other things, too. In particular, Heidi developed a taste for moldy compost heap pickings and breadcrumbs that had been scattered for the birds. Our cat's food bowl had to be placed on top of the dryer so that the poor feline would get an occasional morsel of nutrition.

My husband Jack is an astronomer, and we soon learned that Heidi shares his taste for stargazing. When Halley's Comet was making its return, CBC Television asked Jack for photos to be used on David Suzuki's *The Nature of Things*. Jack only had original slides, and sent them off to the station to be copied and returned. Months passed. Jack and I were walking along a stream on our property one sunny winter's day. We saw something reflecting the sun. Bending down to retrieve what we thought was trash, we found bits of slide film—or rather, *tiny* shards of slide film. Over the next ten minutes, my hyperventilating husband determined the forensics behind our find. A quick phone call confirmed that the CBC had returned the slides to us by FedEx weeks earlier. Since we hadn't been home, the courier had hung the envelope in a pouch from our front door handle. Our dog had obviously secreted them to the lower forty and then patiently pulled every single slide out of its sleeve, then chewed them beyond recognition.

She was also sneaky! I once prepared a tray of fancy hors d'oeuvres in anticipation of a visit by a journalist and set them out on the coffee table just as the doorbell rang. I wasn't at the door more than thirty seconds when I heard a slurping sound from the living room. I glanced up just in time to see the swipe of a long, pink tongue flick across the table, collecting the last of those delicacies.

We also shared strange incidents with our neighbors over the next several years. Heidi was the Big Dog of the Mountain. Spayed shortly after we got her, she nonetheless established her seniority by attempting to hump the male dogs on our street. Her first victim was the goofy Rottweiler who lived next door. Once she had conquered him, it was time to show domination over the pit bull a few houses away. Brutus wore a studded collar and was feared by all—but Heidi showed him who was boss in pretty short order!

Then there was the beagle named BJ who lived next door. They shared a completely different dynamic. It took no time at all for Heidi and BJ to become best buddies. We tried to keep our dog contained, but we were no match for her. The moment we opened the door, she would launch forward like a coiled spring and make a break for freedom before we could grab her. If she made it to the end of the driveway before we could catch her, then she would slink along on her belly to ensure that she stayed out of our line of sight, often disappearing for days. Any hint that we were looking for her would result in her going underground ... literally! She would crawl through narrow, mud-filled culverts, emerging on the opposite side of the road looking like a dirty pipe cleaner. At eighty-five pounds, she seemed to defy the laws of physics when she maneuvered her sausage-shaped carcass through these pipes.

We eventually discovered that Heidi's most troublesome adventures coincided with BJ's. When both dogs were on the loose, they loved to terrorize henhouse and barnyard occupants far and wide. What to do? With the help of our neighbors, we set up a schedule. Whenever BJ was untied, we would lock Heidi up. On days when Heidi was free, BJ would be secured to a clothesline with a long leader. We thought we'd struck upon a brilliant plan until we heard that our precious pooch had figured out how to use her teeth to undo BJ's collar buckle.

BJ's owner, Greg, came by for a visit one afternoon. As he was approaching the front door he spied some plaid fabric sticking out from some leaves near the sidewalk. "Interesting," he said to us when we opened the door. "I have a shirt with that same pattern." For my part, I was surprised to learn that cloth was growing in our yard. I walked over and tugged on the piece of cloth, and out came the remnants of Greg's shirt. And his socks. And his mother's blouse. Heidi had pulled their clothesline down and buried a number of the clothing articles on our ivy-covered front slope.

At this point, I was ready to bury *her*!

But whenever we were angry, Heidi could turn on the charm. Every time I looked into those devilish eyes, I forgave her trespasses. I was hesitant to take her to obedience school in case the mischievous spark I loved was extinguished.

My next thought was to take her to an animal behaviorist. As luck would have it, the famous British dog trainer Barbara Woodhouse happened to be visiting Victoria to demonstrate how even the worst-behaved canines can be cured of demonic habits in five minutes or less. When I described my pet to her, she said the only way to deal with Heidi was to have her put down. The nerve! After that, I stopped inviting Heidi to "go walkies" because that was "Woodhouse-speak."

Heidi was also an Olympic-caliber jumper. This was especially true when my elderly friend, Rita, was anywhere within pouncing distance. Every day, Rita liked to walk almost a mile to pick her mail up from a nest of boxes at the end of the road. My dog's idea of keeping my friend in shape was to lie in wait in the ditch and then ambush her when she least expected it. One December morning we awoke to hip-deep snow. I saw Rita trundling down the road. Swaddled as she was in heavy clothing and earmuffs, she couldn't hear my warning yell. Suddenly she found herself being propelled backwards into a snow-filled ditch. I ran as fast as I could to rescue the poor lady, but arrived too late. Rita was sprawled on her back, limbs flailing, as Heidi stood on her chest and applied enthusiastic licks to her face. As I extricated my friend from the ditch, I was alternately apologizing and cussing at Heidi.

But Rita just laughed. She said it was the most affection she'd received in years.

Heidi loved to ride in the car. She'd stick her head out an open window, relishing every moment that her ears were streaming sideways in the wind. The problem was leaving her in the car if we had to run errands. If we left her unattended for more than thirty seconds, we'd return to find that she'd eaten through one or more seatbelts. We once tied her outside the car but forgot to close the side window. We returned to find that she'd jumped back inside and devoured both rear belts. For ten years, every car we traded in was either missing seatbelts or sported ones that I'd stitched back together with fishing line.

Heidi was never allowed to ride in Jack's prized Pontiac Fiero, since he refused to let her use it as her personal chewy-bone. But we discovered scratches on its hood after it had sat unused in the garage for a number of months. We pondered long and hard how the marks could have been made. However, we once peeked through the garage window in time to see Heidi peering back at us from her perch on the car's roof. She slid down the hood rather like a sea otter slides into the ocean. Her activity level, even in her old age, left us breathless.

You must be wondering what redeeming features this animal could have possessed that would cause me to mourn her fifteen years after her death. I've known lab owners who've had to replace furniture so badly chewed that a three-room grouping was reduced to sawdust. Another acquaintance had a gentleman visitor who stood up after taking afternoon tea with her. It readily became apparent that her Labrador had chewed both of the man's pant legs off below the knee! This same dog tore big holes in the wall-to-wall carpet of the woman's living room, necessitating a multi-thousand-dollar replacement. But in every case, the owners continued to grieve years after their dogs had died.

If this seems strange to you, then either your surname is Woodhouse or you've never owned a lab. These creatures always forgive and are rarely in a bad mood. They expect nothing from you other than a bowl of food and a pat on the head now and then. They don't argue. Plus, they're good judges of character. Heidi was smart enough to bite my scumbag brother, saving me the trouble of doing it myself! Say what you will, but the fact that these canines care enough to give you a concussion in their haste to lavish affection on you is the best welcome home you could ever receive.

Tonight I'm raising my glass to Heidi and all the other yellow labs who rock our world. Long live man's (and woman's) best friend!

Alice and her husband Jack live in BC's beautiful Okanagan Valley. Their home is an astronomy-themed bed & breakfast, where guests often find themselves engaged in conversations ranging from UFOs to string theory. Many hilarious stories about running the B&B found their way into her first book, Tales from Around the Table. *You can visit Alice at **www.jacknewton.com**.*

Duck Heist

Finding a friend in the strangest of places.

By Lee Rawn

During a Winnipeg winter, everybody power walks with their heads down in a familiar no-neck hunch. One can see vapor puffing through scarves as people rush with single-minded determination between heated havens.

Pushing through the door at the University of Manitoba, my stone-cold face met with that pleasing line of temperature demarcation, when minus-forty collides with plus-twenty degrees Celsius. As I pulled back my parka hood, a delicious warming tingle blanketed my face.

I had come to the university to view the science fair. Several of my friends had projects on display. As I walked around I could see an enthusiastic crowd hovering around a table outside the psychology department. Worming my way to the front, I found a box of tiny yellow and brown ducklings.

The tightly packed box was filled with the fuzz balls, peeping frantically as they milled about in their tiny universe. As I watched, one feisty duckling climbed on top of his siblings, his little orange feet bopping from head to head. He quickly reached the lip of the box and catapulted to the table below.

I scooped up the escapee with the intention of returning him to the box, but I first lifted him for a closer inspection and we regarded each other. A wave of affection ignited my heart. Realizing that I was momentarily alone at the table, I lifted the hood of my coat and gently placed the duckling into its warmth. I could feel him settling, pulling my hair over him like a blanket.

Some might call this a duck heist, but I prefer to think of it as a rescue mission. We hurried out the door, waited a brief five minutes for the bus, then rode back to my house. During the bus ride, a little duck head emerged from my hood. Several people gaped in surprise when they spotted the fuzzy hitchhiker. He remained calm, snuggling against the side of my face as he viewed the passing landscape.

"You brought a duck home?" My boyfriend Gary sounded surprised as I untangled tiny feet and wings from my hair.

"His name is Jeremiah," I said. I had recently seen the movie *Jeremiah Johnson* and thought the name worked well for a duck. "Don't worry, I'll take care of him."

We shared the house with another couple. I probably should have asked how they would feel about a new roommate, but it hadn't occurred to me. In any case, they accepted Jeremiah. With a face like his, who wouldn't?

I set up a little fenced pen in the basement and supplied water and food (duck starter from the feed store), warm blankets for sleeping, and a light bulb for extra warmth. But most of the day Jeremiah was with me. Being so small, he usually rode in the breast pocket of my shirt. If I had to go out for groceries, he claimed his usual spot inside the hood of my parka. We chatted during the day (I did most of the talking), and over time a loving friendship developed.

As he grew, my shirt pocket became too small to hold him. When I stood over the sink to wash dishes or cooked at the stove, Jeremiah would sit between my ankles. I kept my feet close together to afford him a comfortable perch. At other times, he followed me from room to room. I carried a rag to wipe up any mishaps.

My little duck was growing up. His voice lost its soprano peeps, and he began speaking in quacks. Every morning, when the mail arrived, Jeremiah would alert me. He would then follow me to the door and burst from between my feet, quacking up at the delighted postman. Jeremiah displayed excellent watch-duck qualities.

At mealtime he would patrol the floor under the table, moving from person to person to beg for food. If we weren't quick enough, he would butt against our legs with his head. We were all vegetarian, so the fare satisfied his appetite. He feasted on lettuce, rice, and a variety of vegetables.

Then there was bath time. Jeremiah would pad back and forth on the lip of the bathtub. Nightly bathing became our habit. I went first, for obvious reasons. He waited impatiently for me to get out and run cold water to cool down the bath. I cleaned the tub thoroughly every night.

One night he became impatient. As I lay immersed in the bath, he shifted from foot to foot, extended his neck, and suddenly dove into the water. A string of duck poop ribboned from his hindquarters into my bath and I leapt from the tub.

"No, no! You have to wait for the cold water!"

But it was too late. The steaming bath had washed away the natural oil that coated his feathers. I lifted Jeremiah from the bath and wrapped him in a warm towel. His soaked little body shivered. A heating pad under his blankets helped, but it took several days to regain his protective coating.

I waited for his striking green head to develop, but as he grew I realized that Jeremiah was more accurately a Jemima. *She* had deep purple markings on her wings and a soft brown-speckled body.

When spring arrived, Gary and I decided to return to British Columbia. We took a few weeks to pack and during that time I tried to accustom the duck to car travel. She would sit on the passenger's seat and, every so often, without warning, her head would shake and an arch of vomit would spray across the dash. The poor thing was carsick.

I had trouble myself with carsickness. I opted for the front seat whenever possible, and would stare straight ahead to cope. But Jeremiah was too short to see through the windshield. Hoping she would adjust, I continued to drive her around the city. For convenient cleanup I kept an old towel on hand.

One day as I was driving along Corydon Street, I saw a young woman hitchhiking. I slid the duck closer to me and stopped to give her a ride.

"Thanks," she said as she jumped in. Then: "Hey, it's a duck."

"I'm trying to get the duck used to car rides," I explained. I should probably have been a bit more specific, as the woman gave me a wary look.

When we reached Osborne Street, Jeremiah puked on my passenger's lap.

How could she not have noticed he was about to heave? I wondered. Scooping up the towel, I vigorously rubbed her pants.

"Let me out," she shrieked. She bolted from the car before it had fully stopped. With regret, I realized that Jeremiah could not handle the trip.

Gary and I drove her to the outskirts of Winnipeg to a duck reserve managed by Ducks Unlimited. The park ranger, who lived in a cabin on the site, told us that his job was to monitor the comings and goings of ducks and to prevent poaching.

"This is the tamest duck I have ever seen," he said. He reached down to give Jeremiah a head scratch. "I will be glad to keep her with me. If she decides that she wants to join the other ducks, she will likely fly south with the flock. If not, I'll look after her. Don't worry. She's in good hands."

We left with both relief and sadness.

Now, many years later, I sometimes watch as flocks of mallard ducks from a nearby lake drop by to gorge themselves on fallen apples in my yard. Once, after a heavy snowfall, the untouched and shriveled apples fell from the uppermost branches to dot the snow, and a hardy flock of ducks glided in from the lake for an easy meal. They landed next to the tree, thus avoiding the fresh ridge of snow left by the plow.

The fruit must have fermented, for the flock's collective waddle was soon more pronounced. After a satisfying feed they flew away—all except one. She continued picking at the apples.

When she was finished her meal, instead of flying (perhaps she was too inebriated), she walked unsteadily back toward the lake.

While she struggled up the snow bank, both feet slipped out from under her and her head disappeared in the snow up to her shoulders. Orange webbed feet waved frantically.

Laughing, I reached for my coat and ran outside to assist. But she had already squirmed her way out. It made me think of the many goofy things Jeremiah had done, and my heart ignited once again.

Lee Rawn is the author of The Solstice Conspiracy, *a young adult novel. She is also known for her comedic short stories. At the Word on the Lake Writers Festival, she received an award, presented by Arthur Black, for her short story performance piece.*

*Rawn often reads to an audience and can quack well enough to summon a flock. You can visit her at **www.leerawn.com**.*

Binkie's Day Out

How to make your sister's cat hate you.

By E.R. Yatscoff

I closed the trunk on the last of my sister Elaine's possessions, which I had agreed to transport across town to her new apartment. "Anything else?"

"Can you take Binkie with you?" Binkie was her orange cat.

"Sure, I guess I can. He doesn't mind riding in the car?"

"He loves it," she said as she pushed him through the open window of my car. "He likes to sit up on the back seat and look out the window." She handed me the key to her apartment. "I'll see you over there shortly."

Binkie did what my sister said he would do. He went straight for that spot by the rear window. I thought it was pretty cool having a cat back there, like some kind of plastic dashboard Mary or hip-swaying hula dancer.

Binkie was asleep by the time I passed the King Car Wash—the first automatic car wash in Edmonton. A sign out front advertised:

SPECIAL TODAY: $1 MIRACLE WASH

I knew that the car wash had enjoyed a splashy grand opening recently, and that the owner had been quoted in our local newspaper as saying, "You have to see it to believe it." And word around town was that it was living up to the hype. Everyone seemed to think it was the best car wash ever. They spoke of its fabulous swirling brushes and how their vehicle was nearly dry when it came out. My shiny muscle car had a thick coating of winter mud and sleet on it. I didn't get to this part of town very often—and a buck to turn my vehicle shiny again was a decent price—so I swung around and drove back to the parking lot.

A pair of tattooed guys brandishing steam wands met me at the entrance. They swept the wands across the bottom of the car, removing large chunks of ice-hardened mud from the wheel wells and rocker panels. Steam rose around the windows.

I glanced in the mirror. Binkie was gone from his perch. I leaned over the seat and saw him lying behind the passenger's seat, tail whipping back and forth as it thumped against the floor. He glared up at me.

"Hang tight there, kitty. It'll be over soon."

The conveyor track jerked a few times and pulled the car inside. I opened a newspaper as the car wash brushes scrubbed my wheels with a deep rasping sound. That was the part most people talked about. My whitewalls would be cleaner than ever. Quite simply, it was amazing and very impressive technology. Unfortunately, this automaton had probably replaced at least a dozen people.

A deluge of water from above splashed onto the roof like a small waterfall. Tall scrubbers beside each front fender spun like tornadoes as their red strands lashed my fenders.

It was all Binkie could stand.

In one vertical leap he was up and on my shoulders, his yellow eyes threatening to pop from their sockets. Claws sank into my flesh as torrents of water blasted the windows around me. I screamed and cursed as I reached up to grab him. He bit my hand and leapt onto the dash, where the view was of a horizontal blue spinner revving up in a turbine crescendo, scrubbing the hood as it headed toward the windshield.

Desperate to escape, Binkie bounded over the headrest and into the backseat … then back onto me again, his teeth and claws fully extended.

I held up my newspaper to beat him off, but he charged through it and slammed into the steering wheel, then staggered to the floor and collapsed. I opened the newspaper and placed it over the cat, as I'd seen them do on wildlife programs. There was no way I could back the car out, and opening my door to signal an attendant would have resulted in an interior wash. I sucked on my bleeding hand, hoping that Binkie would stay down and ride it out. I hadn't seen a NO CATS ALLOWED sign at the entrance. If we got through this in one piece I might suggest posting one.

A truckload of soapsuds dropped onto the car, creating a whiteout. The scrubbers returned for a second, whipping against the vehicle.

The newspaper rattled as Binkie rose from the dead.

He went into a spin cycle, galloping around the car's cramped interior, desperate to escape. He braked on the back of my head, claws digging in solidly against my temples. In the mirror, I saw my bleeding face and Binkie's utter terror. I worried that he might claw my eyes out.

I tried to pry him off. No luck. I rolled down my window, hoping that it might save both my life and the cat's sanity.

Bad idea. I got pasted by spray and soapsuds. Binkie turned a sudsy white.

Modern technology was having its way with us. A huge aluminum box with rubber rollers as wide as my car dropped onto the hood and began blowing hot air. The windshield wipers vibrated as strong winds blew the suds everywhere.

Binkie reached sensory overload and finally extracted his claws. He launched into a frenzied orbit: headrest to backseat to door to dash … then right toward my face.

I put my hands up and ducked.

He winged over the steering wheel and out the open window, and thumped awkwardly onto the concrete floor. Like a cartoon cat, he recovered and skittered on his claws as he shot out the exit.

The large dryer stopped. It was finally over.

An attendant walked over. "Was that your cat?" he said.

I wiped suds from my ear. "Not anymore."

"Pets can get pretty excited in there," he added. "We should put up a sign."

"Yes … yes, you should."

Thankfully I didn't get cat-scratch fever, but I did have to wear a toque for a while.

I also had to tell my sister what had happened to Binkie. I decided to give her a partial rendition of the truth, and told her that Binkie had escaped when I rolled down the window at a stoplight. She wasn't as upset as I thought she would be.

When my sister returned to scrub down her old apartment the next day, she heard Binkie meowing at the door.

The next time we saw each other, Binkie and I locked eyes. It was a look that seemed to say, "Next time I'll drive!"

*Edward Yatscoff is a retired Edmonton fire rescue captain who has created the only Canadian firefighter hero (that he is aware of) in his juvenile ebook series. He describes these stories as tales of old-fashioned true grit and reality. He also guides a writers' group in Beaumont, Alberta, and has published travel articles—one of them a prizewinner—and won a Young Adult writing award. You will find more of his entertaining short stories at **www.yatscoffbooks.com.** The experience with Binkie happened in 1973.*

Hobby Farm

Peace of mind that money can't buy (at Holt Renfrew).

By Lois Gordon

I have no idea how I ended up living on a farm. I blame it on my husband Leif who heard the call to get away from it all, to experience the stimulating challenge of living off the land, to be a pioneer in the verdant farmland seventy kilometers north of Toronto. He tried to convince me that I heard the call too, but I'm pretty sure I was shopping at Holt Renfrew at the time. In any case, the next thing I knew we'd traded in our luxury car for a pickup truck, our manicured lawn for open pasture, and our gas-fired furnace for mountains of cordwood. It's really all a blur, now.

Once settled on our little hobby farm, though, we did manage to immerse ourselves in country life. Our first outing was to the local Co-op, where we picked up matching quilted flannel jackets, hats with earflaps, and rubber boots. Then we read every how-to book about raising fruits, vegetables, and livestock that we could get our hands on. We planted a garden and built a henhouse for a half-dozen leghorns. By autumn, we were well supplied with eggs and ample quantities of produce. In fact, our appetite for home-grown zucchini waned long before our inventory did. As time went on, our family grew to include sixteen chickens, seven ewes, five cats, four pheasants, three peacocks, two llamas, one rooster, and a dog. Our pantry was bursting with canned homegrown tomatoes and herbs hanging to dry from the beams along the kitchen ceiling.

Now, it's not like we were *real* farmers. What separates real farmers (let's call them Group A) from hobby farmers like us (we'll call them Group B) is the way they look at animals. Group A just doesn't understand Group B. Sure, Group A cares about the welfare of their flocks, herds, and gaggles. But they are completely pragmatic about the place those creatures' occupy in the food chain. Cold as it may seem to the uninitiated, when an animal is past its best-before date, well … who needs an extra mouth to feed?

Group B? The first thing they do is name their "babies": Daisy Mae, Duck-Duck, Sweet Pea, Ram-a-Lamb, Chicken Little, and Hen-Rietta. This habit tends to leave Group A scratching their collective heads and wondering, in whispered conversations at the Co-op, exactly what kind of grass the Bs have growing in their pastures.

Leif and me? Group B'ers and proud of it.

To be sure, there is nothing cuter on God's green earth than a baby lamb. Only problem with them is that they grow up, and there's a good reason the boys are called rams. It's one of those words that serve as both noun and verb. You can love rams, you can cuddle rams, you can feed rams apples from your hand; the one thing you *can't* do is turn your back on them. Little Ricky, Clod, Spot, Lamb Chop, Raffles, Mince, Scout … let's just say that each one of them left their mark on us. They're all gone now (may I suggest a nice Bordeaux with your lamb chop?), but not forgotten.

But then there was our baby girl—Tipper—a preemie lamb, so named because her little cloven hooves were not fully developed at birth. With her spindly legs unsupported, she would simply fall over. Her embarrassed mother soon turned her back on Tipper and devoted herself to caring for Tipper's robust brother, Stew.

Into our house came Tipper. (You're starting to get the whole Group B thing, right?) We fitted her with custom-tailored, extra-small Pampers, and set her in a playpen beside the woodstove. Every few hours Tipper had to be bottle-fed and have her nappy changed, and would be allowed to prance about the kitchen while I puttered. We bonded, Tipper and I, and it wasn't just my rubber nipples she was attached to. There was real affection between us. The only moment of unpleasantness happened when she changed the channel while I was watching Oprah. Apart from that, we became as close as conjoined twins.

Needless to say, it tore me up when I had to go back to work in the city. My friend Ineke graciously offered to become a lamb nanny, so every morning I would pack up Tipper's wet nurse formula, her diapers, the playpen, bottles, Vaseline, and soft wipes, and stuff her inside my coat for delivery to my friend's home. Although my lamb nanny assured me that everything would be fine, I found myself overcome with guilt.

My baby! Would she get enough exercise? Learn baaaaad habits? Come home with potty mouth?

One night Tipper managed to clear the side of her crib and gallop down the hallway, her tiny hooves clattering on the hardwood floors.

"Maaaa, maaaa," she cried outside our bedroom door.

After three attempts to contain her—and three more gallops down the hall—I convinced my husband to let her into bed with us. It's not like there wasn't room for her.

Despite my husband accusing me of overindulgence and general weirdness, Tipper and I developed a new bedtime routine: cookies and milk at ten, lights out by ten-thirty. She would get up at midnight for a pee, then turn three circles and lie back down. After a week and a half, she was hitting the snooze button. But it was only when she started hogging the pillow that I realized Tipper had to return to her roots.

Tipper's barn mates made strange at first, but once the scents of fleecy sheets and Baby's Own had been replaced with *eau d'agneau*, Tipper was accepted into the fold. I continued to bottle feed her until she was weaned (let me tell you, she was a bit pissy about that!), and to this day she still takes the time to greet me when I come into the barnyard.

But then we had Little Ricky, another lamb rejected by his mother. It's amazing how kids born from the same parents can be so different.

One day Little Ricky ran out to greet me on the driveway. I realized that he must have led a barnyard breakout: there were two female lambs gamboling in the flower garden, while three others grazed in our vegetable patch. Gloria was resting in a nearby cedar grove, while Sprite got drunk on dandelions.

I cringed when I saw that Ricky had been playing in the mud. Dressed in my designer suit, I didn't want the little guy pawing at me. I adored him and all, but I knew what he was going to do: poke his head between my legs. As far as he was concerned I *was* his mother—the giver of milk, ear rubs, and unconditional love. He never did figure out that his bottle was not attached to my belly.

I sighed. These babies had to be penned up before they decimated our garden. I carefully picked my way past droppings on the driveway to check the barnyard fence. Ricky followed me slavishly, heading for you-know-where and some fresh Wet Nurse. I found the gate ajar and the latch snapped off. Apparently, Ricky wasn't going to let a little forged metal stand between him and my baby bottle. He must have barreled through the fence looking for nourishment.

"Come on, sheepies," I sang. "Let's have some *o-o-oats.*" Like rats following the Pied Piper, the sheep galloped into the yard and I quickly closed the gate behind them.

Ricky made it back through before I had a chance to secure it, but I could deal with one renegade. After all, he was practically potty trained. I knew he wouldn't go far. He cooled his heels in the mudroom while I changed into old clothes; then he attached himself to the inside of my thighs as I made my way back to the barn.

Getting eight skittish lambs into a barn is a lot like trying to scoop up egg whites with your hands. Just when you think you've got them, they slip through your fingers.

Five went in, only to come out again. I coaxed them back. All eight went in … and straight out the hog door. Then they circled around and went back in. I beat them to the hog door and closed it tight, but while my attention was elsewhere they exited through the main door. Six went back in, but four did a quick about-face and once again joined their mates outside. I opened the door, coaxed four inside, and six came out. (Sheep only *look* stupid.) Finally, all but two of them were inside and I slammed the door shut.

I had a plan.

Opening the door to the chicken coop, I tempted the escapees with the promise of lay mash, which is to sheep as chocolate truffles are to humans. They barged past me, startling the chickens. But in the end I fooled them.

"Hah!" I cried. "Got ya!" I'd already emptied the feeder because lay mash, like truffles, isn't particularly good for the diet.

I grabbed for Princess and she bolted behind the straw bales. Daisy followed. I leapt over the bales and grabbed little Princess. We thrashed, we gnashed, we fought hoof and nail, and I don't know which one of us was wailing louder.

I finally managed to grab her and hold on.

One down. One to go.

I crouched down and waited for Daisy. She trotted out and I pounced like a sleek tigress on a gazelle. She screamed, but the battle had already been won.

By the time my breathing slowed to a normal rate, the little darlings were all lying down, contentedly chewing their cuds and gazing up at me nonchalantly.

I fell into the house looking like Scarecrow from *The Wizard of Oz*, peeled off my

Clothes, and dropped them into the laundry basket. I brushed the straw from my hair and took a long bath as I wept over my manicure. I doused myself with Chanel No. 5, which is preferable to *Eau de Barn.* For those precious moments I was the City Mouse again, the woman who never asked for livestock in the first place.

The one who agreed to scramble the eggs as long as she wasn't expected to gather them first.

Wearing silk jammies, I sipped chilled Chardonnay from a crystal glass. Handel's *Water Music* played on the stereo, calming my soul. I sat back to survey my surroundings. The sun was low in the sky, leaving golden streaks upon the pond and illuminating the graceful willows and birch trees with fiery rays. I heard the crickets and tree frogs chirp, and watched birds roost on nearby branches. I thanked God for this blessed idyll, for the beautiful sunset ... and for the skunk that was systematically digging up our lawn in search of grubs.

I think I'll call him Fred.

*Lois Gordon is an author, shepherd, city mouse, and interior designer. She lives on a hobby farm in southern Ontario with her husband Leif and a menagerie of farm animals. At no point in her previous life did she ever expect to look forward to a barn dance, but there's little time for regrets now. For more of Lois's humor stories, visit her online at **www.loisgordonwriter.com**.*

Grizzly Situation

Beware the woman with the cast-iron frying pan.

By Matt Jackson

It was a beautiful summer morning at the Two Jack Lakeside campground in Banff National Park—the sun was shining, whisky jacks were flitting through the air, and the ethereal turquoise of the lake seemed to glow from within. Madge Brown was one of the campground attendants for the national park, and it was mornings like this that made her grateful to be working in such a place.

Two Jack Lakeside campground is one of the closest campgrounds to Banff townsite. Madge's job was to sit in the small kiosk at the campground entrance and provide people with permits. But if any problems arose—problems with noise, or encounters between human visitors and the park's wild residents—she was generally the first person on the scene. For that reason, when she wasn't sitting in the kiosk, she patrolled the seventy-site campground to make sure that everything was in order.

Two Jack Lake sits in the middle of the Bow River Valley, which is a primary migration corridor for all kinds of wildlife— elk, mountain sheep, wolves, and bears. In the 1970s bears were a common sight around campgrounds, so nobody made too much fuss about them. Black bears in particular were a dime a dozen, and were often seen along the Minnewanka road that connected Two Jack Lake to Banff townsite, or even in the campground itself. Unless a bear started poking its nose into a camper's personal belongings, the park's unofficial policy was to leave them alone.

So it was that Madge was sitting in her kiosk on this perfect morning, only to be interrupted by a loud banging at the door.

When she opened it, she found a large woman standing in front of her with a scowl on her face. The woman was wearing an apron with a full bib; in one hand she carried a broom, and in the other, a large cast-iron frying pan.

"Y'all gotta come and do something 'bout that bear!" said the woman. She had the unmistakable accent of a resident from the southern United States.

"Excuse me?" said Madge. "You've seen a bear in the campground?"

"Darn tootin' I have! He's rippin' ma tent apart, goin' through all ma food, and messin' up ma dishes!"

"What does the bear look like, ma'am?"

She fixed Madge with a withering gaze. "He's big and brown is all I kin tell ya," she said. "I done hit 'im with ma broom, an' I hit 'im with ma frying pan, and he just will not go away!"

"You hit him with your frying pan?"

"I most surely did!"

Madge suggested to the woman that they drive to the campsite to investigate. Sure enough, when they arrived, they found a large grizzly bear pawing through the remnants of the woman's supplies.

"Look at 'im!" said the dismayed woman. "He's just ruinin' everything!" She got out of the truck, waving the frying pan above her head, and prepared to do battle once again.

"Uh, ma'am. Please get back in the truck!"

The woman looked startled. "Excuse me?"

"I'm sorry ma'am, but that's a grizzly bear. It would be a very bad idea to hit him with your frying pan."

Sitting in the truck with the brooding woman, Madge called the warden service with her radio, and within a few minutes they had arrived on the scene. By then, the grizzly had wandered off into the forest, so the wardens were forced to evacuate the remaining campsites and close down the campground.

Later that day, two wardens managed to find the bear again. It was no longer in the campground but had stayed in the general vicinity, and for that reason the bear still posed a threat to public safety.

As the wardens stepped out of the truck to better observe the bear, it immediately turned and charged at them. By some twist of fate they had left the truck doors open, so they were able to quickly dive inside and yank their doors shut, even as the grizzly crashed into the side of the truck like a huge furry missile. Over the next few minutes, the bear charged at the truck repeatedly, smashing its head against the metal frame again and again. By the time the bear was done, the truck was demolished.

Madge doesn't know what eventually happened to the bear, but the campground didn't stay closed for too long.

She did, however, have to console the angry woman, who had to pack up her damaged tent and broken dishes. The woman was particularly incensed that the park service had stood idly by while the grizzly bear destroyed her campsite. She had been fully prepared to offer the bear a dose of his own medicine.

Matt Jackson is a professional writer, editor, and the owner of Summit Studios, a Canadian publishing company that specializes in books about travel, humor, and the Great Outdoors.

Shoplifter

The mysterious case of the missing underpants.

By Mary Patterson

"Guess I need a new windbreaker."

My husband's admission surprised me. Fred usually has to be dragged to the men's wear store, protesting loudly that his favorite coat is "just starting to get broken in."

Looking at the article in question, I suspected that he'd been wearing it when he was out on one of our tracking trials with our basset hound, Sam. One of them had apparently decided the fastest route was close to a barbed wire fence. In fact, on closer examination, it looked like he'd actually gone through the fence! There were slashes all the way up one sleeve, which had exposed the red lining.

As my husband's sense of color coordination leaves much to be desired (an ailment many husbands possess, or so I'm told), I quickly threw on my own jacket and said, "Why don't we look for a new coat at Chapman's?"

Sam the Basset, sensing an outing, was at the door in a flash—or at least what passed for rapid movement in an eighty-five-pound dog. As usual, Sam chose to block the doorway with his long, narrow body—a barricade too high to step over comfortably. He turned his head up and rolled his eyes toward his leash, which was hanging on a hook beside the doorframe. Sam's long, floppy ears gave him an almost mournful appearance.

"Oh, all right," I muttered. "I suppose you can come with us." I put the collar around his massive neck and led him outside. "But we're only going shopping," I warned him.

Sam didn't care. He was happy to go anywhere with us.

Our neighborhood men's wear store—Chapman and Sons—has been in business for years. Like many family-run businesses, the owners welcome both man and beast, and Sam is a favorite of theirs. Sam wags his tail for everyone, and with his longtime weight problem, he has never been one to jump up on people.

As we sorted through the jacket rack, Sam pulled away from us. He stretched out comfortably on the doorway carpet.

"How about this blue one?" asked Len, one of the store's owners.

"Is it dog slobber proof?" I asked.

"Hmm. Maybe you'd better try this washable gray one instead," said Len.

Fred put it on and struggled to do up the zipper. "It's too tight. How about that light brown one?"

"Dry cleanable only," I told him.

As we continued our search for a new jacket, I glanced over at Sam to make sure that he was behaving himself. He was sniffing along the edge of the men's underwear display rack with the curiosity that bassets possess, but everything seemed in order.

A jacket was finally selected and paid for, but as I picked up Sam's leash I saw a tiny white sliver protruding from the side of his mouth.

"What have you got there?" I said as I leaned over. "Come on. Spit that out." Sam's huge mouth opened to reveal a pair of white cotton briefs, still neatly wrapped in their cellophane covering. I pulled out the package—and my wallet—and apologized. Now that they had been drooled on, I would surely need to pay for them.

"No need," laughed, Len. "See? There's no damage. I'll just give the package a little wipe." As he reached for a paper towel, he added with amazement, "Imagine him being able to fit that entire package in his mouth!"

When I looked down I saw that Sam seemed to be chewing on something. "Just a moment," I said. I pried Sam's mouth open and pulled out a second package of underwear. "We're lucky," I said to my husband as I read the label. "They're your size."

My husband pulled out his wallet, too. But Len once again waved away the offered payment. "Bad Sam! What were you thinking?"

Sam responded by rolling his huge eyes up, which exhibited a picture of canine innocence.

As we opened the shop door to leave, something—lets call it a mother's instinct—made me kneel down and look Sam straight in his eyes.

"Open up," I demanded, and with great reluctance the mouth once again opened wide. I reached far down into the large red cavern and came up with a third set of briefs—this pair carefully unwrapped!

"Thief!" I scolded.

The three of us looked at each other and started to laugh. Then a thought came to me. "Where do you think he's stored the wrapper?"

But Sam never told us that part.

Mary Patterson is a longtime garden correspondent for Toronto community newspapers who recently switched to creative writing. She had a short story published in the Wild Words *anthology of the WCDR, which mused about the funny side of life with urban raccoons. She and her husband are potters, gardeners, and lawn bowling advocates, but are especially fanatical about basset hounds, whose sad faces hide their clown souls. Mary is currently finishing a mystery novel set in Toronto's High Park, with murder by mushrooms as the theme. And yes, a basset hound is one of the characters.*

Darth Robin

A bird schooled in the dark side of the Force.

By Freye Parkhouse

Nothing had prepared me for the evil robin. As I awoke with spring's light entering our bedroom window, with birds in song on the budding branches, he was lurking on the porch railing downstairs. Bears had sauntered through the woods of our mountain abode; deer, birds, and squirrels made their homes among us; raccoons had been shooed away from the cat's door. But nothing had prepared me for him.

I should have noticed something in his bearing that foretold of his inimical acts to come, something reflected in his maniacal eye and puffed-up, defiant stance. But I only saw a herald of spring, an omen of the unfolding season.

I was startled when he began throwing himself against the living room windowpane. He seemed crazed: again and again he returned to the railing, only to fly into the window with renewed ferocity. My curiosity at studying a robin at such proximity soon vanished and gave way to concern. With such intent and velocity, surely he would knock himself out. Theories began to seed themselves.

"Go on you. You're going to kill yourself," I admonished, rushing outside and shooing him away. "Go on, you fool."

He moved back onto a tree branch and observed me from his own distinct frame of reference. I returned inside and began to sip my tea when I turned to observe him with his wings extended, trying to climb the pane. Theory two: He was not misguided, but demented.

I figured that through deductive reasoning and by process of elimination, I would find out what was wrong and solve the problem before my wife returned in a few days. I supposed that, if he wasn't crazy—which wasn't to be ruled out—he might consider this area some kind of thoroughfare. I taped a large towel against the window to signal the obstruction. The robin stared at the towel. Pleased with myself, I made my way upstairs.

When I reached the top floor I looked outside and saw the robin flapping madly, like someone treading water. He hovered outside my study window with his eyes pinned on mine. It was becoming personal.

To be honest, I was stunned. Had I entered a Hitchcock movie? Or had I suddenly acquired the ability to communicate with birds? Perhaps I could be a future ambassador for their species, pleading their case to humanity. My new business card:

FREYE PARKHOUSE

ANIMAL COMMUNICATOR

SPECIALTY: ROBINS

I wandered back outside to make myself available for the first interspecies communication, but my mystical experience was not forthcoming. He eyed me for a moment, then hopped a short distance away.

"Hey," I said encouragingly. "There is nothing here for you. You're welcome to the birdfeeder, but there's just no reason to knock yourself out like this."

Back inside, the incessant sound of bird hitting glass returned.

I opened the door and ran across the porch. "Get out of here, damn it!" I shouted. He sat on a nearby branch and stared at me defiantly.

I walked back inside. The towel I had taped to the window had fallen down. I gathered several available magazines and newspapers into a stack and began taping them to the inside of the window. This deterred him somewhat, but inevitably he returned to his behavior. I then taped paper to the *outside* of the pane. After some hesitation, he began to attack the uncovered window next to it. After I covered that one, he continued on to the next one. There were breaks in the action when he must have left to feed and nurse his wounds. In these intervals I regained my composure and hoped that it had all been an aberration. But always he returned. By nightfall, half of the lower-floor windows were covered in old newsprint.

The next morning the robin arrived at five thirty. He seemed unscathed. I clearly needed help. When the hour came I called B.E.A.K.S.—a bird sanctuary—and waited nervously as the line rang.

"This is B.E.A.K.S.," said a voice.

"Oh, hi. I have a question about the unusual behavior of a bird—a robin actually. I'm not sure what to do. I'm wondering if you can explain the behavior."

"Is he attacking your windows?"

"Yes. How did you know?"

"Oh, many people think robins are such nice birds, but they're actually quite aggressive and territorial. He sees his reflection in your window and thinks it's another male robin, so he's attempting to drive him off."

"Ah … an explanation. I thought he might have eaten some poison or something."

"No, no. A lot of people think that the bird is cracking up. The females should be here soon. Once they start mating, they start to care less."

"I can understand that. I thought it was me … I just started putting up paper."

"That's it. Paper's the best. Put it on the outside of the window though."

"Well, thank you. It's such a relief to have an explanation."

"Good luck."

Knowledge was the key to everything. Now my methodical, logical side could go into operation. It was just a question of papering the windows. And so I went—room to room, window to window—with my stack of assorted papers and masking tape. But the robin was always one step ahead. If I left a piece of paper improperly attached, he would appear from behind the paper with his menacing eye and begin his assault on his elusive adversary. Magically, his enemy always avoided his attack at the last moment, only to reappear when the Evil One withdrew in the illusion of victory. At which point, he would throw himself with greater vigor against the pane.

There were times when impractical theories seeded themselves in my tired brain. At one point I decided that I would catch, cage and drive the robin far, far away. Or just cage him until the females arrived.

I tiptoed along the porch with a towel in hand, turned the corner of the bay window and met his steady gaze. He timed his escape perfectly—taking flight at the moment of my throw. I went inside and opened all the windows, hoping to trap him inside the house. He alighted on the window ledge and teased me with a disinterested look.

A primeval emotion suddenly rose from the pit of my stomach up into my head. "Aargghh!" I screamed. I grabbed a broom and raced outside, flailing it wildly at the bird. He hopped placidly from branch to branch, and with a curious eye regarded this example of human behavior. It felt like I was in a cartoon. Stunned by the realization of how thin the veneer of civilized behavior is, I walked back into the house, opened a beer, and resigned myself to the process at hand.

It continued for two more days, me with my tape and papers and the robin in pursuit of his elusive foe. Finally, I had finished covering every window in our home with newspaper. Outside in the sunlight, the robin circled the house. Now I was surrounded by a host of celebrities hitherto unknown, who stared back at me from the open newspaper pages. But at least the incessant, infernal crashing had ceased.

By the time my wife Portia returned, I had become used to the absence of daylight. It was a small concession for the truce that I hoped would lead to his perceived victory and, therefore, his eventual departure.

"Boy, you weren't joking. This is unreal," she said. "It's like a tomb in here. Oh well, maybe he'll go away and we can be back to normal in a day or two."

Of course, he did not go away. He continued his surveillance.

"I can't take this anymore," my wife finally said. "There's no light in here. We've got to figure something out. I'm beginning to hate that bird."

So we plied the Internet for strategies. One site claimed that robins do not like helium balloons, aluminum foil, or wire screens. We tried both the balloons and aluminum, but they were a short-lived novelty for him. I then placed bubble wrap along the deck railing in a spiteful act, hoping that when he landed they would pop. But he nimbly continued his "robin runs" without deterrence.

Next we purchased a roll of synthetic black screen from the local hardware store and tacked it to the outside of his favorite windows. That buffered his blows and allowed a small amount of natural light to return. But the gray metallic screen was our salvation, as it allowed even more natural light into the house. It was simple, inexpensive, and above all, effective. We rolled it out, measured, cut, and tacked it up. And he did not like it one bit. Perhaps it offended his touch; or maybe his archrival seemed to be disappearing into the mists. The light poured in and the windows were protected. Darth Robin had been deterred.

When we were sure he had gone, we took the screens down. Clear light filled our rooms and peace descended upon our domain once again. However, the robin did visit us one last time while our plumber was coming up the driveway to fix an outdoor spigot.

"Do you have a bird problem, ma'am?" asked the plumber when Portia came outside to greet him.

"Yes, we do," she said matter-of-factly.

"I thought so. I saw this robin. I couldn't believe it! It flew right into one of your windows, almost like he was attacking it!"

"That's him all right," Portia answered with a resigned tone.

"I can get rid of him in no time with my pellet gun," the man offered.

"Oh, no, we couldn't do that. We love animals," said Portia.

There are those who will believe we went too far in accommodating the robin. After all, he is just a bird—a rather dense creature that can't even recognize his own reflection. But before we take too condescending a view of our spring herald, we should reflect upon our own beliefs and how they have shaped our behavior. For instance, we believed for centuries that the earth was flat and that the sun revolved around us because it looked that way. But it turned out that was merely an illusion.

We can only hope that our robin will eventually "get it" and realize that those other would-be robins, hiding behind the shiny surfaces we call windows, aren't robins at all.

Freye Parkhouse lives and writes in the mountains just outside Nelson, BC. He has now placed a heart-shaped mirror on the railing of their deck so that any male robins that return to his home can quite literally "knock themselves out."

The Masked Intruders

They might be cute if they weren't so gosh darn annoying!

By Jan DeGrass

They come by night. They break, enter, and shamelessly steal our food. They wear black masks and have sharp teeth, sporting nimble fingers that end in Dracula claws.

Yet for some reason humans find them cute!

In my experience, raccoons are nothing more than a ruddy nuisance. They weigh up to twenty-five pounds and possess wide fat bottoms and ample haunches suitable for jumping to upper sundecks. It was this latter characteristic that, at least in the past, had prevented them from entering our house through a small cat door.

Not this year. A slim-hipped, silent intruder managed to wriggle through a door designed for a cat half its size, breaking the plastic flap in the process. Forensic evidence suggested that, once inside, the creature ignored the spitting and hissing of the resident cats while at the same time gnawing through a large bag of Friskies. It washed some of the food in the cats' water dish, then enjoyed a snack before removing more food through the hole in the door, presumably to share with its raccoon cousins.

Of course, after the raccoons discovered that premium cat food makes their coats shine, the family dispatched the slender commando on more missions. She returned night after night, waking us at various ungodly hours—at midnight, 2 a.m., or 3:30 a.m. Her arrival was always marked by an unmistakable thump as she swung over our porch's railing and landed on the deck. This was inevitably followed by the howling of cats and gnashing of feline teeth as she entered the house. But in the distance, the bandit was cheered on by what sounded like verbal applause coming from her family.

It was difficult to catch her in the act. She made a speedy getaway each time, until one night she paused to study the vertical blinds hanging beside her escape route. When she discovered they were quite tasty, she lingered for a reflective chew and was most annoyed when I shooed her away, shreds of fabric still hanging from her teeth.

The battle began in earnest.

"I'll scare her away," said my husband Will, who had been an urban dweller most of his life and who admitted that he had never seen a raccoon at close range. That night, at the first sound of incursion, he armed himself with a striped golf umbrella and—dressed only in his robe and slippers—charged onto the porch yelping karate cries. It's difficult to say whether the raccoons or the neighbors were more amused.

"Why don't we use the hose?" I suggested. I coiled the hose by our bedroom's sliding glass door and adjusted the nozzle to "jet stream." For the plan to work I only had to wake from a sound sleep, get out of bed, find my glasses and the flashlight while shivering in the cold night air, pick up the hose, and then aim it and spray a hard stream of pressurized water at the culprit until she scampered away. The plan had one fatal flaw: I was doomed never to have a good night's sleep again. After attempting this plan repeatedly, I always seemed to wake up drowsy and have to drag myself through the day. The raccoons, for their part, didn't seem to mind.

I soon learned that having a raccoon is a little like having the common cold. Everyone has a remedy.

"Leave them a peanut butter sandwich," suggested my friend Marlene. "It gums up their mouths, which they don't like. They won't come back."

I was skeptical.

"I'm serious," she repeated. "What would it cost you to try?"

Marlene's advice seemed to contradict the official literature from the local conservation branch, which told us to lock up all food sources. So we cleaned the cat saucers, foamed the area with carpet cleaner, removed the blinds and packed the cat crunchies away in Tupperware containers.

It's conceivable that the raccoon family had long been hosting Tupperware parties in the trees, because the concept of sealing food inside an airtight plastic container was no mystery to them. If the intruder's long claws could not open the container right away, she dragged it to the door—where, we imagined, several larger raccoons selected by the clan blasted the top off with tiny sticks of dynamite. The latter part is speculation, based on the mess we were usually forced to clean up after the fact.

"Why don't you use pepper spray?" asked my mother. She added that she didn't think she would be visiting just now, dear, until I had solved the problem.

While speaking to a friend whose house borders on wilderness, I explained how my sleep was being disturbed by the nightly prowler.

"We don't have raccoons in Sandy Beach," she told me. "The cougars prey on them." This seemed like the perfect solution—wild predators restoring the population balance—until she casually mentioned that no domestic cats had been left alive either. There was also the problem of where to find a few good cougars.

I was becoming desperate.

"I've got it!" said Will. "Let's take the bedside lamp, remove the bulb, turn the lamp on and plant it inside the cat door."

I vetoed that idea on the grounds that I didn't want to clean a charred raccoon from the porch. Instead I spoke with a neighbor. Had she been bothered by the raccoons?

"Not like last year," said Donna. "Joe built a trap and we caught thirteen of them. Would you like to borrow it?"

After seeing the trap, it was clear that it would have been suitable for Rambo of the raccoon world. Built from scrap wood and thick wire mesh, it was three feet wide and rose to just under my chin. It had an elaborate system of elastic bands that secured the food to the floor so that the animal was forced to climb inside to grab the bait.

"Just so you know, once you catch them you can't leave them inside the cage all night," Donna warned. "They go crazy." She advised us to load the cage onto a truck and drive them out to Port Mellon. "Joe released them all in the same place so that they would be able to find each other again."

Unfortunately, this seemed an even better way to disturb a good night's sleep. And more to the point, we would have to borrow a truck from Marlene, who still insisted that peanut butter sandwiches were the best solution.

"The longer this goes on, the fatter that animal will get," Will suggested. "Then she won't be able to fit through the door." We decided to wait for a little while longer, using the hose deterrent whenever feasible.

One night, during a 3:00 a.m. incursion where I made more noise than usual, I woke up Will in the process. For some reason we both continued to stand in the doorway, watching groggily as the creature scampered just outside of the hose's reach. As we continued staring into the night, the raccoon came back with another larger raccoon that danced forward for his turn in the shower. Thus refreshed, they began to play, wrestling on the lawn in a friendly fashion, as frisky as two newlyweds under the moonlight. Tired but fascinated, we could only watch from the doorway.

"Are they mating?" asked Will.

"No! Please don't say that!" I exclaimed with eyes bleary and glasses askew. "We don't need any more little raccoons."

"Look honey, they're just playing," Will continued. "Aren't they *cute*!"

Jan DeGrass is an award-winning writer and editor who pens a weekly arts column for The Coast Reporter. *Her first novel,* Jazz with Ella *(Libros Libertad), is about a Canadian Russian language student who travels to the Soviet Union in 1974 and meets a discontented jazz pianist who desperately wants to leave the country. She has also written a corporate history book and a cookbook titled* Take Potluck! *She lives on the rural Sunshine Coast in British Columbia.*

Horse Play

Stick out tongue. Pull. Retract. Stick out tongue.
Pull. Retract.

By Diane Stringam Tolley

I was raised with horses. OK, I'll admit that I lived in a house and our horses were quartered in the barns. But we *did* spend an inordinate amount of time together.

For anybody familiar with horses, I'm sure I don't have to tell you that they are smart and that every one of them has a distinct personality. Some horses are lazy. Some are crafty. Some love people. But there is one universal quality they all share: horses love to play.

Not surprisingly, horses left too long in a stall will get bored. Some resort to entertaining themselves by chewing on the walls and/or gates, or kicking said walls and/or gates. A bored horse can figure out many different ways to make a nuisance of himself. For this reason, considerate owners sometimes hang old plastic jugs or pull toys for their precious pets to play with. But what these overgrown puppies really prefer is a bit of your time. Oddly enough, most are quite easy to entertain.

One of my favorite horse games as a child was called "tongues." It's played by tickling a horse's lips until he sticks out his tongue, whereupon you give it a little pull. The horse takes this as his cue to pull it back into his mouth.

Then he promptly sticks it out again.

Stick out tongue. Pull. Retract. Stick out tongue. Pull. Retract.

They love this game. Most horses can play it for hours. Or until you get tired of it. You can probably guess which scenario usually happens first.

In the mid eighties, the province of Alberta was in its heyday of building museums. Many world-class repositories were erected to house collections of period cars, old machinery, airplanes, dinosaurs, natural resources, natural disasters, and rocks. You get the picture.

One of these museums—not surprisingly—was built to revere and/or elucidate the role that the horse played in the settlement and development of Alberta. And my husband Grant was in charge of said building. During the early planning stages of the project, he was sent to Britain to tour any and all museums housing a similar collection. As he had mentioned the word "horse," I decided to tag along.

We were nearing the end of our sojourn and were touring the Buckingham Palace Mews, led by none other than a man named Edward—the head hostler to the Queen. He was a very proper and pleasant man.

Edward and I hit it off immediately, as it was clear we both loved horses. With the Queen and her entourage "not in residence," Edward had been able to show us over the entire facility. We had been escorted, dutifully and happily, through the coach storage buildings, the wash racks (a dirty horse isn't allowed in the Buckingham Palace Mews), and the feed barns.

Did you know that pedigreed royal horses eat the same food as our Canadian prairie mixed breeds? They do. It just costs more and comes in prettier packaging.

We finally reached the stables—ah, heaven!

I should also mention that horses are intensely curious. If something is happening, they want to be front and center—gawking and getting in the way. Many will pretend to be startled and flee spiritedly, only to come back and see if they missed anything.

For the resident horses, our tour of the royal stables was something out of the ordinary, and thus deserved every ounce of attention they could provide. As we walked the length of the building, heads popped out of stalls one after another. One horse, a handsome gray gelding housed more or less off by himself in a corner loosebox, seemed especially interested.

As we passed, the big gelding leaned over and sniffed me. I sniffed back, then started to move along. He nickered softly and moved with me.

I realized that he was probably bored, so I reached out and touched his lips. He licked them. His tongue was momentarily exposed, so I reached out and pulled it.

His head shot up, startled.

He stared at me for a couple of moments while his horsey brain worked through what had just happened. Then he stuck out his tongue again. I pulled it. He drew it back in. Then he did it again.

This went on for some time. Grant and Edward had been standing a little ways off, talking, and the big gray and I had been enjoying our game so much that I hadn't realized the stable had fallen silent.

I turned. The men were watching us. Thinking they had finished their conversation and were waiting for me, I patted my new friend and started toward them. The big gray leaned out as far as he could, nickered at me, and stuck out his tongue, as if to say, "Hey! I'm not finished with this game!"

I laughed and patted him again before joining the men.

Edward was still staring at me when I approached. He shook his head and in his perfect English accent said, "In all my years, I've never seen a horse do that before!" He looked at me with renewed interest and said, "Any time you want to come back here, you are more than welcome. Anytime."

I smiled. A horse lover knows another horse lover.

More than anything, I learned something from our royal experience. It's not that all horses have the same 'horsy' breath, which they do. And it's not that they all have the same wonderful "horsey" smelling hide, which they also do. It's that all horses are simply *the same*. No matter what social circles they move in.

Diane Stringam Tolley was born and raised on the Alberta prairies. Daughter of a ranching family of scribes, she inherited her love of writing at a very early age. Trained in journalism, she has penned countless articles and short stories. She is the author of five ebooks and the recent Christmas novels Carving Angels *and* Kris Kringle's Magic *by Cedar Fort Publishing. She and her husband, Grant, live in Beaumont, Alberta. They are the parents of six children and grandparents of thirteen.*

Jambon

Somewhere, an accordion began to play.

By Steve Pitt

I once did a cooks' tour of France with some fellow trainee chefs. Being the only non-teenager in the group, after a few days I felt the need for at least one meal without being asked to "Pass the salt, dude." I finally got my chance in the town of Beaune where, owing to a one-day French bus strike, we unexpectedly found ourselves with half a day to wander around on our own.

I immediately snuck off for a solitary lunch. In a matter of minutes, I found a picture-perfect French restaurant, complete with waiters in handlebar mustachios and starched white aprons the size of China clipper mainsails.

The regional specialty of Beaune is escargot. Well, who can resist a chance to eat snails? A half-liter of wine and a basket of crispy still-oven-warm bread arrived first. One bite, one sip, and I was ready to put down roots for life.

After a few minutes, a striking, well-dressed woman in her late thirties entered the restaurant twirling a cigarette holder in one hand and a leash on the other. At the end of the cigarette holder was a lit cigarette. At the end of the leash was an ancient boxer (the canine variety, not the pugilist sort). She called her dog something like "Jambon," and it waddled painfully behind her like a dutiful sugar daddy. In France, cigarettes and dogs are still allowed in restaurants. The dogs generally smell better.

Madame took a seat at the nearest table with her back immediately to me. Jambon dutifully settled down under her chair. Already waiting for her was a young man in his twenties wearing a badly wrinkled Harris Tweed coat and shiny black pants. He was sporting the worst comb-over I have ever seen.

Being France, it could have been l'amour, but more likely it was just an elegant woman lunching with her dorky stamp-licking bureaucrat nephew. Whatever the reason, the one thing they definitely had in common was smoking. As they chatted incessantly, huge clouds of smoke rolled my way. Just so you know, French cigarettes smell like burning mummies.

Being Canadian, I endured it in silence. Besides, I was geared up for my escargot.

For those who have ever dined on escargot in North America, please note that the rubbery, pathetic little overpriced slugs they serve there bear no resemblance to the homegrown variety of Burgundy, France. In most North American restaurants, snots (trade name for snails) come in cans. The contents are heated in a microwave, stuffed into pre-owned snail shells, then given a deep-sea burial in a greasy sauce, usually from the same can.

In France, escargots are picked fresh from the field, detoxified for forty-eight hours, cooked in their shells, then covered in a super-rich garlic-butter sauce. Because these snails are still anchored to their homes, the French have invented special tools to evict them. You get a spring-and-claw thingy that grabs the shell like a surgeon's clamp, along with an elegant two-pronged pick that you stab into the meat and pull.

The waiter slid a dimpled dish bearing six escargots in front of me with a flourish, bowing and snapping a napkin. Being a complete novice at snail-picking, it took me at least a minute to grasp the shell in my clamp, jab in the pick, and slowly but firmly pry my first juicy escargot out of its shell.

I raised my impaled snot to find that I was not dining alone. Smelling food, Jambon had abandoned his station at the foot of Madame's chair, jumped up on the chair opposite me, and commenced ogling me and my lunch with a love-struck stare that you could find only in France.

I cleared my throat a couple of times, trying to get the attention of Jambon's owner. When at last she noticed my phlegmy hints, she did nothing more than contemptuously light another flaming Tut.

Ignoring Jambon's unblinking gaze, I chowed down on my first snail. Indescribable, the way that garlic butter hits you. I stabbed into my second one. Jambon, perhaps thinking that somehow I hadn't noticed him, emitted a low whimper of sweet longing that would have done Maurice Chevalier proud. No dice, Monsieur Bow-Wow. The second escargot met the same fate as the first.

Escargot number three put up a fight. Or maybe my hands were just a tad shaky because Jambon was now talking to me. Or at least he was opening and closing his mouth and making "maa-maa-maa" sounds, punctuated by longing moans. So call the French SPCA; I ate the third snot, too.

At escargot number four, Jambon must have decided that I just couldn't see him through the clouds of purple smoke. So he slammed his huge head on the table with a loud thunk, jowls fanning out on each side like pancakes. Snail fork poised in the air, I made the mistake of looking him in the eyes. Huge, brown, unbelievably sad eyes. Somewhere, an accordion began to play. A tear seemed to form at the side of one of Jambon's eyes and his lips stretched in a long black line nearly eight inches across, quivering as if they were about to break out in heart-rending sobs.

I couldn't stand it! I served him a quick snot on a piece of French bread. He gobbled it down in one bite and then looked hopefully at the remaining two snails.

Damn, I thought. I just realized that I had set a precedent. Fortunately, the first three escargots had been incredibly filling, so I decided we could split the difference. I gulped down the fifth snail, then picked up a six-inch stick of French bread, smeared it end to end with the last of the garlic butter, and topped it with the final snail. Without dropping so much as a crumb, Jambon took the baguette out of my hand and tilted his head back. In one motion, the bread slid out of sight with the band still playing "Nearer My God to Thee."

The food gone, Jambon abandoned his chair and returned to his place under his mistress. Not so much as a thank-you. Not even a backward glance. Harrumph. The French. I finished my wine, had dessert and coffee, received and paid the bill, and got up to leave.

Just then, both Madame and companion simultaneously stopped chatting. They wrinkled their noses in horror and scanned the restaurant for the offender.

They glanced at me, but I was too far away. They glared at their nearest neighbors, who protested their innocence. Finally, they looked under the table at Jambon, who was asleep. His tail and toes twitched as if he was having a dog dream. It wasn't a dog dream.

Madame and her table companion wrinkled their noses once again, the waiter flapped his apron, and everyone else dabbed their eyes with their napkins and complained to Madame about her dog. I assumed my best Gallic snoot and headed for the door.

Time for a little fresh air, dude.

Steve Pitt has been a professional writer for more than 30 years. In 1980 he won a Periodical Distributors Author's Award for humor for an article that appeared in Harrowsmith *magazine. In addition to being a writer, Steve Pitt has worked as a movie extra, army reserve soldier, dishwasher, farm hand, martial arts instructor, bartender, youth outreach worker, armored truck guard, Yukon gold prospector, manager of a shelter for homeless men, goose rancher, lay minister, bar bouncer, resort cook and stay-at-home dad. You'll find him in cyberspace at* **www.stevepitt.ca.**

The Heifer

Say howdy to one thousand pounds of enraged, adrenaline-laced bovine!

By Trevor Reeves

"This could get messy," said my friend Jack. "Are you game to help?"

"I suppose so."

Jack kicked at a frozen pile of cow manure. "I never should have bought these heifers. They're as wild as moose and just as ornery. Can't get within forty feet of them." He explained how one of them had rammed his good rope horse when he was trying to drive her into the corral.

Jack had called me late the previous night. He had a pregnant heifer with one foot showing out the birth canal. Forty years of ranching and three weeks of experience with those heifers told him that this was a job requiring some veterinary assistance. Not only were the heifers wild; they had been bred to a bull that was producing calves too big for them to have without help. So here we were—Jack and I—staring at the heifer while she alternated between staring at us and careening madly around the outdoor corral.

"We need to get her into the barn," said Jack, shivering in the morning chill. "Once I open the barn door I'll park the truck lengthwise on the far side of the entrance. If you stand behind the truck and hold up that piece of plywood, it will block her escape route. I'll push her along the fence until she has no option but to run inside the barn."

Of course, there are always other options. She could turn and charge at Jack, or even smash into the fellow holding the plywood (me). It's fair to say that this was not a good plan, or even a good idea, but there really was no alternative.

Much to our delight, once the barn door had been opened, the heifer took one look at us and vanished inside the barn. I darted over and slammed the door. Success! Now we only had to enter a confined space with one thousand pounds of enraged, adrenaline-laced bovine and slip a rope over her head, while at the same time managing to avoid a crippling injury. Piece of cake.

"What do we do now?" I asked.

Jack considered our options. "How about you distract her while I slip into one of the pens on the far side of the barn? When she charges at the pen, I'll rope her."

Jack had about a twenty-foot run across the barn floor, followed by a five-foot leap over a wooden wall to get to safety. My job was to get the heifer's attention and momentarily preoccupy her with trying to kill me rather than him. I was to accomplish this by running to a low dividing wall on the near side of the barn. The wall was roughly ten feet long and attached to one end to the barn wall, so it divided the closest wall of the barn into two equal spaces. Once there, I planned to jump from one side of the five-foot wall to the other, always keeping the wall between me and the heifer. Once the heifer had moved to the end of the barn furthest from the door, Jack would sprint to the pen.

Again, this was neither a great plan nor a good idea. But in the cattle practice of the 1980s, it was probably fairly consistent with the way things were done.

Our plan went surprisingly well, with the exception of Jack almost getting his trailing leg shattered as the heifer slammed into the wall of the pen as he scurried over the top. With Jack safely in the pen, I climbed on top of the five-foot wall, balancing myself by holding on to one of the wooden pillars that anchored it to the ceiling. The heifer spent the next several minutes bluff-charging both Jack and me, until Jack was able to throw a rope around her neck. He then threw the free end of the rope to me.

I tied the rope around another support pillar near the barn wall. Several more near-death experiences later and we had the heifer snubbed to the pillar. Now she had only a narrow space bounded by the wall of the barn and the low wall I had been standing on to maneuver. By pushing into position a freestanding metal fence panel, and using some rope to tie it to the low wall, we had her secured.

"That sure went well," said Jack, beaming. He used his teeth to rip off a torn and hanging fingernail fragment before limping over to retrieve his hat.

"Yes, that was easier than I thought," I replied. I rubbed my shin where she had kicked it and squeezed my index finger to staunch the blood where the skin was torn off.

I used an epidural to freeze the heifer's hind end before examining the birth canal. I could immediately see the problem. One of the calf's front legs was stuck behind its body. Without both legs and the head in the birth canal, the calf was wedged. I reached in and managed to find the foot, cup the hoof with my hand, and then manually pull the calf's leg into position. I attached the calving chains so we could pull on the calf's forelimbs and help the heifer with the process. There was a brief moment when it seemed the calf was too large for a natural birth and that a cesarean would be necessary. But then the calf slid free and plopped onto the straw of the barn floor. We moved the calf off into one corner. I quickly checked to make sure there was only one calf, then gave the heifer a shot of oxytocin to shrink the uterus and prevent a uterine prolapse.

Lou, Jack's wife, came in just before the calf was born. Once it was obvious there was no need for warm water for a C-section, she told us she would put some coffee on and see us inside the house. Jack and I were preoccupied with the calf and didn't pay much attention as she left. In particular, we didn't notice the ominous clicking sound as she closed the barn door.

Now it was time to release the heifer. This was supposed to be the easy part. We just had to ensure that we were well out of range when she finally got her freedom. She would be looking for somebody to punish for the abuse she had suffered. Our plan was to utilize the freestanding metal fence panel by attaching it to the end of the low wall so as to fence her into the far side of the barn. Then one of us would release the lasso and we would walk briskly, but without a care, out the barn door.

The plan went flawlessly. To a point. And that point was reached when I put my hand on the barn door and pushed. The door didn't move.

I looked at Jack with horror and said, "It's locked!"

At that same moment we heard the sound of the fence panel being kicked over.

Jack and I sprinted back to the low wall and vaulted over it with the heifer in hot pursuit. A few mad moments of jumping back and forth over the wall—frantically alternating our positions relative to the heifer—and we finally managed to climb on top of the wall.

However, we now had another problem. Standing on the wall was fine when I was standing on the wall and Jack was inside the pen. She couldn't concentrate all of her time and energy on one task. Now she could, and quite soon she was going to start trying to knock us off the wall. The distance between the end of the wall and the pen was about eight feet. It was too far to jump, and the heifer was either occupying or watching that gap. Our only hope was the calf. If it started to bawl, the heifer would go over and check on it. Hopefully her maternal instinct would kick in and she would become obsessed by her calf. That would allow us to cross the corridor and climb the fence into the pen.

Sometime later—I think it was only slightly less than the age of the universe—the calf began to move and make some noise. The heifer, as predicted, went over to check on it. Now was the time to make our move.

I jumped off the wall. Then I jumped back on. The heifer was not as preoccupied with the calf as one would wish. As soon as she saw me hit the ground, she charged. I had to abort my mad dash for the pen and instead run for my life alongside the five-foot barricade, then back up onto the wall that Jack was standing on.

Now it was time for Plan B. Which was actually Plan A. There was no possible Plan B.

So it went: Attempt Plan A. Run for our lives until we could climb back onto the wall. Wipe sweat from our foreheads. Repeat.

Eventually, the heifer was distracted by the calf just long enough for me to attain the wall of the pen and quickly scramble up and over. Now I was inside the pen and Jack was on the wall. Step two was for me to open a hatch in the barn roof. The hatch closed a hole usually used to drop hay from the storage space on the top floor of the barn to the lower floor. However, this presented a new problem. The hatch was not over the pen. It was about four feet to one side, and as a result it was out of arm's reach, even when I was standing on the wall of the pen.

I searched the pen and found a pitchfork. Using the pitchfork, I was able to push the hatch open. But now I had a new problem. There was no earthly way I would be able to climb out of the pen and sprint across the floor to the fixed ladder. The heifer would reduce me to mincemeat. The only option was for me to jump, catch the edge of the hatch with my hands, and pull myself up and through to the top floor.

As you can imagine, this was another really stupid idea. If I slipped, I would drop onto the barn floor and be trampled by the heifer in seconds. But it seemed the only choice, so I took a few deep breaths and made the jump. With my good friend adrenaline to help me, I shot through that hole like a porpoise.

The remainder went without a hitch. I opened the outside door in the upper part of the barn, climbed down another fixed ladder and opened the barn's main door. Lou had dropped the bar across the door on her way out, something she had done every day for forty years. It was force of habit.

As soon as the door opened, the heifer saw her chance and shot out of the barn. Close on her heels was Jack. Without hesitation, Jack and I jumped inside the truck and slammed the doors shut. We drove across the corral to the closed gate. We looked at each other for a moment, but etiquette dictated that the passenger (me) open the gate for the truck to pass through. There wasn't really any danger from the heifer; she was as sick of our company as we were of hers.

When we arrived at the farmhouse, Lou nonchalantly asked us why we had taken so long. I think Jack had a sharp word to say. I don't recall. But for some reason, the coffee tasted particularly good that morning.

Trevor Reeves has practiced as a veterinarian in the Peace River District of British Columbia for twenty-nine years. He believes that if something doesn't kill you it makes you stronger. He also believes that well-marbled, three-inch-thick New York steaks barbecued rare, potato salad, and beer is the optimal diet for any human being.

Pet at Your Own Risk

May I have my thumb back please?

By Greg Simison

It appears my daughter feels that having three cats and a dog isn't enough, and for that reason a new puppy has recently been added to the menagerie currently filling her house. I suppose I shouldn't blame her, since her most recent boyfriend bought it as a surprise, and though I don't know what her reaction was, it certainly surprised her other pets. I don't know why this new guy didn't settle for something requiring lower maintenance—like a bouquet of flowers or a box of chocolates. At the rate she changes boyfriends there could be trouble if they all began doing this. If it keeps up she'll soon have to start looking for a kennel to house them all. The pets, not the boyfriends—though some of them look like they'd be quite at home in a cage, or on the end of a leash.

The problem with this new addition to her family is it has resurrected my son's interest in getting a dog of his own. We've been fighting over this issue for the last year or so, his hopes no doubt fuelled by my ex-wife. Our two cats are definitely on my side since they know as well as I do what sort of monster he has in mind when he uses the word "dog": a combination of pit bull and Rottweiler, bred to be as mean as possible, and probably with a taste for the flesh of stubborn fathers. I'll be doomed if I give in on this.

When he brought the subject up this week I put my foot down once again and told him there will be no dog joining this household while I live and breathe. Judging from the crazed look in his eyes, I wish I had phrased it some other way. Once his sanity returned he announced, "Then I'll move out and get my own dog."

This statement is a perfect example of the completely twisted reasoning of teenagers. I think he truly believes that a threat like this will cause me to change my mind and allow some larger, meaner version of the Hound of the Baskervilles to take up residence with us. If anything, it makes me even more intractable on the subject. Nevertheless, I make sure to leave the newspaper on the kitchen table every morning—opened to the Pets for Sale section of the classified ads, and right beside it a section to the Apartments for Rent. It's a long shot, but it just might work.

Anyway, back to the subject of my daughter's new canine. It's a small dog that could easily fit in the palm of your hand, assuming you'd be foolish enough to put your hand that close to it. Only those who believe that four fingers and a thumb at the end of each arm are too many should attempt this.

From the limited amount of information her boyfriend received from the hunchbacked dwarf who was selling these dogs from the back of a dilapidated hearse, he concluded it is some sort of cross. Personally, I think cross is too mild a word. Very, very cross would describe it better.

Of course, cross could also mean crossbreeding between species. I'd guess it's part Chihuahua mixed with a rodent of some sort, perhaps an extremely lonely gopher or, more likely, a terribly deformed lab rat that recently escaped from a biological warfare lab. If I squint when I look at the thing I can even see a Gila monster with a thin layer of fur on its scales. Shortly after pocketing his money the dwarf was seen driving off, hotly pursued by a team of scientists in biohazard suits.

And she was stuck with the dog.

It's said that appearances can be deceiving. Not in this case. I'd like to report that the puppy turned out to be a loving, friendly little creature, and that all who came in contact with it immediately adored it. Yes, I would like to be able to say that, but to be honest I can't. Its true nature came out about thirty seconds after my daughter brought the puppy into the house and introduced it to her other pets. I call it a puppy. But as with most Chihuahua-like alien life forms that throughout their lives maintain the size they attained three minutes after birth, it could be almost any age—a month, six months, ten years, or a thousand years old.

My daughter placed the puppy on the back of the couch so the three cats and the other dog—a large, gentle black lab/pit bull cross—could approach and get used to it slowly. Big mistake. As the first cat got within range, the new puppy leapt at it and had that old tom by the throat before it could get out a terrified *MEEEOOOWWW!* It then quickly released its grip and managed to tag the other two cats before they could flee. Oh, sure, the puppy took a few scratches across its deformed nose, but I think it could have actually killed all three of those things if its jaws weren't prevented from closing because its mouth was already too full of the fur it had ripped from cat number one.

As for the lab, which had witnessed the assault on its feline buddies, I can only ask if anybody has seen a black dog turn pale? Well, I had never thought it was possible either. It then topped that trick by collapsing into what can only be described as a kneeling position in hopes the puppy would recognize it as the universal sign of submission. After thinking it over, I don't know whether it was a kneeling position it was trying to assume or if it was attempting to form the shape of a crucifix with its two front paws, the sort of sign intended to ward off Dracula or some other approaching horror. Whatever it was trying to do, it worked, and it got off with just a severe beating.

Anyway, it's been a week now and things seem to have settled down somewhat. The black lab (a most inaccurate term, as it's turned quite white in the last few days) has been busy running errands for the puppy, and the cats are starting to heal and relax a little more. The daily dose of a thousand milligrams of Valium the vet has prescribed for each of them seems to be helping.

I'd like to report that my son, after watching the new puppy at its blood sport, has changed his mind about a dog and opted for a gerbil instead. Don't I wish. It seems he has a growing number of enemies and feels that a Chihuahua of his own, closely related to this one, would provide better protection than a .357 Magnum. And damned if he hasn't finally managed to convince me that there may be some sense in this.

"Remember," he said. "Mom's coming to our place for Christmas, and you know the first thing she's going to do when she arrives is pick up any new puppy she sees and cuddle it—real close to her throat."

Hey, who am I to deprive my boy of a dog?

Greg Simison is a writer living in Moose Jaw, Saskatchewan. His fifth book, Miscellaneous Wreckage, *a new collection of poetry, was released by Thistledown Press in 2014. His daughter soon gave up the dog described in "Pet at Your Own Risk" and it has lived with him for the last nine years. They are inseparable. A situation he hopes will be remedied when it unlocks its jaws from his hand.*

A Very Persistent Bear

It's all about knowing your adversary.

By Carolyn Kohler

Just when you think you know everything about traveling through bear country, there's a bear that makes you realize how very little you really know. On a recent backpacking trip, we came face to face with such a bear.

My husband Tom and I had backpacked many times in the Ansel Adams Wilderness of California. It is a stunning area filled with sharp-tipped, glaciated peaks and clear blue lakes, and one of our favorite camping destinations. For this trip we had invited two close friends, Lisa and Adrian, also avid backpackers, and Tom's city wise fourteen-year-old nephew, Jake, who hailed from central (and very flat) Indiana. This was going to be Jake's second backpacking trip, and my husband wanted him to have a great experience in the mountains.

As we put on our packs for the fifteen-kilometer trek, we talked excitedly about the beautiful, untarnished country we were about to enter. We were headed for Thousand Island Lake for four days, and since we would be camping at an elevation of 9,200 feet, we expected to see some snow.

Two miles into our hike, we met up with a weary looking father and son coming down the trail. "If you are going to Thousand

Island Lake, watch out for the bear," they warned. "It got all of our food." We listened to their tale of woe in earnest and offered some of our energy bars to help them get back to the trailhead.

Not long after, we came upon a young man and woman trudging down the trail, so we stopped to exchange information. Their warning echoed that of the first campers we had met: "Be careful of the bear at Thousand Island Lake. It stole our food last night."

We talked briefly about the bear, but decided to carry on. Tom, Lisa, Adrian and I had already made dozens of backpacking trips into bear country. We had pitted our food storage skills against some of the smartest bears in California, and the only incident we'd had was with the infamous car-door-ripping bears of the Yosemite Valley. That experience had made us strict practitioners of the art of proper food hanging—packing one's food in a special bag and suspending it from a high rope strung between two trees, well out of reach of bears. Since then, we had always managed to keep our food safe. So in spite of the sad stories we had just heard, we felt confident that we would be able to outwit this big, bad bear.

As we headed deeper into the wilderness we started to see snow on the ground—much more than we had expected. So much snow, in fact, we could barely find the trail. When we finally reached Thousand Island Lake, not only was there a lot of snow, but the lake was almost completely covered in ice. "No wonder the bear is stealing food," said Lisa. "It woke up hungry from its winter nap and found this."

We walked along the lakeshore and soon found the perfect campsite. It was a level area with a great view of the lake, and it had a tree with high branches strong enough to hang our food from. We set up our tents, with Tom and me in one tent, Lisa and Adrian in a second, and Jake in a third. Tents assembled, we gathered some firewood, made a fire, and then settled in to have dinner. Later, we carefully stowed our food by packing it into two large bags, tying the bags together with rope, and counterbalancing the rope-tied bags across a limb in our tree. We pushed the bags high up into the tree with a stick, certain that they were well beyond the reach of any bear.

As darkness fell, I walked to the lake for a moment of wonderful silence. I looked around the shore and saw no other campfires. *Hmmm*, I thought. *If there is a bear at the lake tonight, it's going to come looking for us.*

Back at camp, I quietly shared that thought with my husband, feeling that there was no need to alarm Jake.

For those of you who are not familiar with California black bears, they are nocturnal creatures that do not like confrontation. Although they might try to steal your food, loud noises and a few well-aimed stones can usually discourage them. Nevertheless, before turning in, I positioned some pots and pans outside our tent flap. They would act as an early warning system in case a snooping bear attempted to poke his head inside our tent.

Everyone was tired after our long hike, and we quickly fell asleep.

Less than an hour later, I was awakened by a noise like the squeaking of a pulled rope. I grabbed my flashlight and poked my head out of the tent. There was a bear not more than thirty feet away, and since I was lying down and looking up, it looked as large as an elephant. Worst of all, it was holding one of our bags of food in its claws and contentedly chomping away.

"The bear has our food!" I shrieked.

In seconds everybody was awake; you've probably never seen a commotion more comical than five people struggling to get out of their sleeping bags all at once. After crawling out of our tents we yelled at the bear, banged pans together, waved our arms, and threw stones. Finally the bear had enough of our food (and of us) and lumbered away into the darkness.

We quickly assessed the situation. One bag of food had been pulled from the limb onto the ground and was badly mangled. The second bag was still tied to the other end of the rope and was high in the tree, untouched.

"How did the bear ever reach the food bag?" I asked. It had to be one very large bear!

We hung our remaining food, this time forming a human pyramid and using a very long stick to hoist the bag even higher. Unless the bear was fifteen feet tall, it would never be able to reach our food. Or so we thought.

We prepared to retire again, but Jake looked worried. "Come sleep in our tent," my husband suggested. Jake looked relieved. I was relieved too, since now I would be positioned between two warm bodies and that much harder to get at if the bear felt so inclined.

An hour passed, and I was awakened again by a new noise. This time it sounded like scratching and scraping. I grabbed my flashlight and poked my head outside the tent. The bear was back, and it was climbing our tree. There are few sights as funny as a very large and ungraceful bear trying to scamper up a tree. I woke my husband and Jake, and we howled with laughter as we watched.

It took a few minutes, but the bear finally made it to the limb that held our food. Then it crawled, ever so carefully, across the very small and precarious limb to the rope that held our bag of food. To our astonishment, it then began hoisting one of the food bags, paw over paw, as if it had hands! In a few seconds, the bear had the bag in its jaws.

By that time we were all out of our sleeping bags, yelling and screaming at the bear. It looked down at us placidly and began munching away.

Seeing that the rope was still tied to the bag and was now hanging low enough to the ground for us to reach it, my friend Lisa decided to engage the bear in a tug-of-war. Lisa is not a fragile flower; at five feet ten inches, she can (and regularly does) bench-press a hundred and forty pounds. Lisa grabbed the rope and began to tug. The bear dug in its claws and tugged back.

Lisa tugged harder. The bear hung on. Finally the rope broke and Lisa fell on her backside. Ah well; it had been a noble effort.

We yelled louder, but the bear continued to eat our food. After a few moments, Adrian decided to capture the moment and ran into his tent for his camera. He began snapping photos and we discovered that the bear did not like the bright flash. In fact, it let go of the food bag and slowly backed down the tree.

An uneasy moment ensued for all of us. Now that we had tormented the bear while it sat on its perch, what would it do? We backed slowly away from the tree and hoped for the best. It seemed to take forever, but the bear finally reached the ground and ran off into the darkness.

What food we had left was now stuck in the tree, and we had no way of reaching it. We decided to go to bed and figure it out in the morning.

You may have guessed what happened next: the bear came back and started clambering up the tree again. It must have been just as tired of fighting with us as we were of fighting with it, because a single flashlight directed in its face made it reconsider. It ran into the woods and didn't come back.

The next morning we awoke tired and hungry, and stared longingly at the bag of food stuck high in the tree. Tom came up with a possible solution: throw a rope over the limb and use it like floss to free the bag of food. With Tom on one end of the rope and Adrian on the other, they worked at the bag of food until it finally fell from the tree.

We looked through the bag to see what was left. The bear must have had a sweet tooth, because all the cookies were gone, along with our hot chocolate mix and our peppermint schnapps. Not only was it a persistent, well-fed bear—it was a drunkard.

After taking an inventory, we figured we had enough untouched food (just barely) to last one more day. We decided to move to a different campsite with no snow and no hungry bears. But as we packed up our gear, we found one more surprise.

The previous night, all of us had leaned our backpacks against a large log five feet from our tent. At some point during the night, the bear had searched our empty backpacks for food, leaving footprints and a telltale trail of saliva. Not one of us had heard a sound. The thought of such a big bear coming so close to our tent gave me the goosebumps.

For recent backpacking trips, we've ditched the counterweighted food-hanging method in favor of a bear-proof PVC canister. We have not had our food stolen since.

As for our nephew, he returned to Indiana with a great story about his "ferocious bear encounter," bringing the mangled food bags with him as evidence. It must have been a positive experience for him, since he now lives in the Rocky Mountains of Colorado.

Carolyn Kohler is a freelance writer specializing in copy writing for websites. She lives in the San Francisco Bay Area with her husband Tom Patterman, with whom she takes every advantage to enjoy the great outdoors. You can reach Carolyn online at: **www. effective-web-sites.com**

Sleeps with Chickens

He was one of my "type-three" friends.

By Sylvia Shawcross

"George, do you know any Sicilians?" I asked. George was standing beside our car wrangling with a bag of peat moss.

We'd just gotten back from the local gardening center, where we'd spent the last two hours attempting to understand the difference between particular types of manure. It's apparently quite important to know the difference between goat and sheep manure if you want to grow splendiferous rhubarb. I know this because a sprightly old man with a great drooping nose spent at least twenty minutes describing how luscious his stalks were last year because of his manure mixture. Needless to say, by the end of it we had felt obligated to pick the right one if only so we wouldn't offend the poor fellow. The last thing we wanted was to get caught slinking out of the place with bags of bargain manure, so we bought the sheep stuff and bags of shrimp compost. Shrimp compost is apparently the best thing *ever* for green things wanting to grow, according to Mr. Nose.

George, still wrestling with the peat moss, was in no mood for conversation. He was sitting on the hood of the car grumbling about how peat moss—seeing that it was *only* moss—shouldn't rightly weigh more than St. Peter himself.

"No," said he emphatically. "I don't know any Sicilians. But if I did I'd make sure they were here to help unload the peat moss."

I myself didn't know any Sicilians here in our small town of Chelsea, Quebec, and even if I did I was quite certain there was nothing I could possibly have done, or written in any of my columns in our local newspaper, to deserve the gift of a dead crow in a bag on my front doorstep.

Except it wasn't a crow. George, when he reached the porch, unceremoniously dumped the limp bird onto the floor and examined it intently.

"It's a chicken," he said. And so it was: a small bird with black feathers.

I was already working myself into a tizzy when it dawned on me. "It was that column where I fricasseed the chickadee, wasn't it?" I said. I knew that column would come back to haunt me. It was satire, for heaven's sake! Why don't people understand satire anymore? It's not like I *actually* cooked the chickadee. And even if I had, whose business was it anyway? I have the right to cook chickadees in my own home if I bloody well want to! It's not like chickadees are on the endangered species list.

And anyway, putting a dead chickadee in a bag on my doorstep would have been more to the point. What kind of enemy was this? If this was indeed a Sicilian death threat, it seemed—I don't know—feeble.

At that point I decided to do what every woman in the world would do—I started phoning my friends.

Now, by way of explanation, I should say that I have three basic types of friends. The first type is likely to know who put the chicken on my doorstep—as well as when and why they did it—because they know everybody's business. The second type of friend will commiserate comfortingly and make me feel like I'm a wonderful human being who doesn't deserve a dead chicken on the doorstep, but will never actually help me solve the mystery of the dead chicken. Unfortunately, I also have a third type of friend. This type can explain in detail how the downing of the twin towers was an inside job and that one-legged pygmies from the South Pole are the ones to blame for the swine flu epidemic. They are also the type most likely to have actually put the chicken on my doorstep.

For this reason, I decided to start by calling all of my type-three friends. Several hours later it dawned on me that I seem to have a lot of friends in that third category, so by the time I'd phoned Fredrik I was more frazzled than a dead chicken. Suffice it to say that I was in no mood for banter.

"Did you deliver a dead chicken to us today, Fredrik?" I asked him point-blank.

"Oh, yeah," said Fredrik sleepily. "Yeah ... I did."

"Fredrik, dear," I said calmly. "Would you please explain why you've put a dead chicken on our doorstep?"

Fredrik, being Fredrik, gave a perfectly logical answer. "I left my big pot on the stove and forgot to turn off the burner."

"I'm deeply chagrined," I said. "Here I was thinking that someone was plotting to kill me. How ridiculous. It's all so obvious now. So let me get this straight: you ruined your big pot so you put a dead chicken on our doorstep?"

"Yeah," said Fredrik.

At this point I probably should have just had a cheery conversation with Fredrik and carried on with my life knowing that at least it wasn't a death threat or a voodoo curse, and was instead just one of my type-three friends going about their business, such as it is. But I was beginning to worry about Fredrik because, as I recollected, Fredrik didn't actually own any chickens.

I don't know why I had to know where the chicken came from. I just did. "Where did you get the chicken?" I asked.

"I guess it came from Mildred's farm across the way," said Fredrik.

"Oh," I said. "So you don't know where the chicken came from?" Call me crazy, but this all sounded rather suspicious.

Realizing from his tone of voice that he actually planned to eat the dead chicken, I said, "And we know this is an fresh chicken because?"

To which Fredrik gave a perfectly logical answer: " Because I stole it from a pigeon hawk."

"OK," I said. "That explains pretty much everything I wanted to know." What this actually meant, of course, was that I didn't want to know anything more, and that I would be happy getting rid of the chicken carcass on my doorstep.

But Fredrik, now wide awake, explained in great detail how he had been on his way to someplace for a very specific reason, and was passing by Mildred's when a pigeon hawk flew past and dropped the chicken in Mildred's front lane. So Fredrik did what anyone would do (at least according to him): he chased off the pigeon hawk and grabbed the now-dead chicken. He called it serendipity. Furthermore, Fredrik now figured the pigeon hawk was his "spirit guide" totem. I asked him how he knew it was the pigeon hawk and not the chicken that was his totem, but he didn't respond.

"You know, Fredrik," I said quietly, in that tone of voice I often find myself using with my type-three friends. "Stealing chickens from hawks kind of makes sense in a strange sort of way, even here in suburbia. But then, it doesn't explain why you dropped the chicken off at my front door. You don't expect me to cook this chicken, do you? There's a reason why chicken comes wrapped in plastic from grocery stores. It's so we don't have to actually know what we're eating. You *do* understand that, right?"

"We should learn how to pluck a chicken," said Fredrik matter-of-factly.

"And why would that be?" I asked.

"It's good, cheap organic food."

"Oh," I said. But I don't think it was very convincing.

After I got off the phone, George asked me about the chicken and I said, "Fredrik burned his big pot." For some reason this was a good enough explanation for George, who then wandered off to find a rake. I'll never understand men.

Of course, this was how I found myself sterilizing an axe, rubber gloves, pliers, and knives on a perfectly good Friday night—because I still had a big pot—when I really just wanted to do the cryptic crossword, have a nice cup of tea, and go to bed. Thank God for *Mrs. Beeton's Book of Household Management*, that ancient tome my grandmother gave me long ago. Among other things, it gave detailed instructions on how to pluck, butcher, and cook a chicken.

By the time Fredrik arrived, the sun was setting and a rich red-orange light flooded the back stoop of our home. Fredrik carefully and painstakingly assembled his chicken-plucking logs in perfect symmetry.

"I think you have to hang the thing from the rafters for a bit," I said, quoting *Beeton* from page 357. "I'm not sure why."

"Nonsense!" said Fredrik, who was wearing a pair of black leather gloves. "Raoul said all you have to do is pluck the thing."

"You need to dunk it in boiling water before you do that," I said, quoting *Beeton* from page 358.

"Nonsense!" said Fredrik, as he cheerfully began plucking the chicken with our pair of pliers. He lectured me on the merits of self-sufficiency, even though I figured I was perfectly happy being self-deficient by purchasing my chicken from the grocery store. I began protesting that in our little town of Chelsea *nobody* killed chickens, and that black leather gloves were not for chicken plucking no matter how you looked at it.

"There has to be a trailblazer in every community," said Fredrik. "Soon everyone in our little town will be slaughtering chickens. It's the new way of things."

"Even Mildred takes them north of Wakefield to have them murdered by somebody else," I offered up feebly. But Fredrik wasn't listening to me anymore. He was trying to pluck the top of the chicken's head.

"I think you're supposed to remove that part," I said, somewhat sardonically. Well, the truth is, my tone of voice was more alarmed than sardonic, because I couldn't figure out why Fredrik wanted to pluck the chicken's head. The feathers are so darn tiny. And it's not like I'd ever run across the need for a chicken head in any recipe, or even going out for dim sum, for that matter. But then, I didn't really want to know why Fredrik was plucking the chicken head, so I watched quietly for a while, thinking about page 354 of *Mrs. Beeton's*, where it explained chicken decapitation in great detail.

Eventually I left Fredrik to his organic evangelism, because the sight of him with an axe bathed in that fiery red glow of the setting sun plucking a chicken head was becoming more than I could handle during my waking hours. When George wandered in looking for dinner I told him not to go out on the back stoop because the Butcher of Seville was out there posing for a Hieronymus Bosch painting, and that supper would arrive eventually in one form or another.

For an hour or so, we both managed to ignore the assorted tortured grunts and groans drifting in the window from the back stoop. But I eventually started worrying about what the neighbors might be thinking. When I wandered out I found a miserable Fredrik mangling the remnants of a chicken-like thing with his bare hands. He insisted of course that skinning a chicken instead of plucking it was a perfectly acceptable form of preparation, not to mention healthy without all that fat. Looking at the half-bald chicken head and the ruined gloves, I figured it was a wretched sight no matter how you looked at it.

The long and the short of it was that Fredrik did manage to make a chicken stew for us. However, as I explained to him, "I have seen the face of the chicken and for that reason can't eat a bite."

George, who conveniently missed the mangling, had two helpings.

Sylvia Shawcross lives in the forested hills of Chelsea, Quebec, but her heart belongs to the Maritimes. She writes a humor column for The West Quebec Post, *and in 2011 she won the award for Best Columnist in Quebec by the Quebec Community Newspaper Association. She is also the author of two books:* Never Mind All That *and* The Get-Over-Yourself Self-Help Book. *In the words of Farley Mowat, she is "that rarity of our times, an honest-to-god satirist." As such, Shawcross loves to rail against the insanity of our world in her unique curmudgeonly style.*

Monkey Business

When a small, furry companion becomes a dictator.

By Rita Pomade

We were an assorted crew sailing out on the China Sea, sprawled on the deck of the *Santa Rita*, chugging down Tsingtao beer and gorging on shrimp chips. The *Santa Rita* was a 45-foot ketch that my husband Bernard and I had built in Taiwan. The crew was made up of some of the colleagues with whom I taught English at the British Council. I had invited them for a day of rest and relaxation aboard our boat.

It was a miserably hot day. A slight breeze offered some relief, but not enough to wake us from our lethargy. Bernard decided to rig a makeshift chair under the boom, which he extended out from the yacht. We took turns sitting on the chair with the wind at our backs and skimming the waves with our toes. It was the only relief we had from the heat.

Most of us were settled into a comfortable stupor, waiting our turn, when Bernard called out that he'd spotted an octopus about ten yards off the stern on the leeward side. Skepticism and the weight of our perspiration kept us glued to our seats. We were far more interested in not missing out on the chair-ride than in whatever flotsam was bobbing around in the sea.

Bernard, an independent soul, took no notice of our lethargy. Despite our protests, he lowered the sails to slow the yacht's speed, jumped into the dinghy, primed its engine, and set off for a closer look at his discovery. He was back in less than five minutes with a repulsive-looking thing slung over the crook of his arm.

My first impression was that the object was a large rat—a waterlogged creature one step from death. Its limp, gray form hung motionless over Bernard's arm like a dishrag. A thick cord was knotted around its neck, a soggy piece of which trailed along the deck.

Ahmad, a Malay fisherman Bernard had invited along, was the first to speak. "It's a monkey," he said. "Maybe drowned."

He walked over to Bernard, took the limp creature from his arm, and laid it on the deck seat. He breathed into its mouth and pumped the little arms. The matted ball of fur gurgled and spit up some water, like a tiny fountain. It opened its eyes and stared at us while we cheered its miraculous resurrection.

Ahmad looked up. "It's a baby, a female," he said. "Maybe six months old."

We moved away to give it some space, but we couldn't take our eyes off the tiny form. "I didn't know monkeys could swim," I said.

"She's a crab-eating macaque," Ahmed said. "They swim." He took a penknife from his pocket and cut through the cord tied around her neck. "She's probably contraband. Monkeys aren't allowed in Singapore without papers. But rich people pay a lot to eat their brains. It's not legal, but people still want them. They're smuggled in from Indonesia. The smugglers must have seen a customs boat and threw her overboard." He turned to Bernard.

"She's been swimming a long time. Probably wouldn't have made it if you hadn't seen her."

The monkey appeared to be listening to every word the fisherman said. She didn't take her eyes off of him, and as he talked, she was growing noticeably stronger. To our surprise, she jumped off the seat and onto the deck—still fragile, but determined. She moved from person to person, chattering nonstop. "I think she's desperate to tell us her story," I said. "Or perhaps she's thanking us." It was hard to know what was going on in that little head.

It was love at first sight for Bernard. He scooped up the tiny body with one of his huge hands and sat her on his palm. "I'm going to name her Lola," he told us. He looked the monkey straight in the eyes, and said, "Welcome aboard, mate."

The savior and agitated ball of fur stared each other down. Neither one blinked. Eventually, Bernard broke into an idiotic grin.

The first night Lola wouldn't stop crying, so we wrapped her in a small blanket and brought her into our berth. She insisted on sleeping between us and fussed if she was pushed to the edge. The first morning of our *ménage a trois*, we discovered that toilet training was going to be an issue. We couldn't walk her like a dog, and she didn't have the fastidious nature of a cat. Our berth was a stinky mess.

We discussed what to do about her dreadful toilet habits. I told Bernard that she was his monkey, and that he'd have to find a solution. He went ashore in search of a box of Pampers.

On his return, he took out a pair and carefully cut a hole for her tail. The Pampers were sized for infants and came up to her armpits, but she was willing to keep them on. I made it clear that changing her was his responsibility.

Lola grew more beautiful each day. Her dull coat began to shine under Bernard's diligent grooming. Then one day she began to groom herself. From that moment on, gratitude was dead. She quickly forgot that she owed us anything. Her appealing, almost modest nature morphed into that of a little tyrant. Lola emerged from her piteous shell to become a spoiled and unmanageable child, given to sneaky thefts and pouting when reprimanded. Worse, Bernard became head honcho, while I was relegated to lowest person on our totem of three. Every time Bernard disciplined Lola, she slapped me hard on the leg.

Lola spent hours grooming Bernard. She inspected every hair on his legs and arms. From time to time she stopped, looked at her fingers, and slipped a speck of something into her mouth. For the life of me, I couldn't see anything and couldn't imagine what she was harvesting.

In turn, he spent hours grooming her, pretending to pick specks off of her coat and putting them into his mouth. It was a ritual that she enjoyed, and it kept her out of trouble for a short time.

On her more expansive days, Lola even groomed me, her nimble fingers inspecting every inch of my scalp. And as she did with Bernard, she would stop from time to time to take some questionable thing off of my head to eat.

After she had groomed me, she would sit on my shoulder and stare at my hand as I wrote. Writing both fascinated and perplexed her. It was always when I was hunched over the little table in the aft cabin, writing in my journal, that she would decide that I was most in need of a "makeover." She never tired of watching me move my hand across the page. Somehow this endeared her to me, and I would momentarily forget what a naughty girl she could be.

Lola followed Bernard everywhere and became agitated if he was out of her sight for any length of time. She could distinguish the sound of our dingy from all the others in the harbor, and whenever she heard him returning from shore, she would dance with excitement and dash up the galley stairs to greet him.

She imitated everything that Bernard did. He rolled his own cigarettes. Lola wanted to roll her own too. She was actually pretty good at it, although I was constantly picking up bits of tobacco and paper. At first I thought it was funny. Then she started handling the matches and the scene lost its humor. Tobacco, paper, and matches were securely locked away. But that wasn't easy, since Lola could open just about anything and inspected the contents of the lockers daily.

Aside from feeding her, everything relating to Lola was Bernard's responsibility. She saw me as an intruder on their boat. I was tolerated, but not indulged. Basically, I was relegated to the dual role of housekeeper and cook.

Unfortunately, all acts of food preparation enthralled her, and I learned that I couldn't turn my back on her for a second. To keep her out of trouble, I fed her peanuts while I cooked. She stuffed them into her cheeks until she looked liked a chipmunk, and then begged for more. When I ran out, she would hide in a corner and take them out of her mouth to be eaten one by one, hidden from my view lest I discover her subterfuge and take the extra peanuts away—or worse, ask her to share.

My status improved when my father-in-law came for a brief visit. There was now a lower person in the hierarchy. So low, in fact, that he was subject to bites after a Lola-Bernard argument. The poor man spent his entire vacation gripping a flashlight to ward off her attacks. When he saw Lola coming, he would bop her on the head. She eventually got the message and kept her distance, but it was an uneasy truce.

During a day's sail to Malaysia, Lola and Bernard had words. The sails were up and a light breeze was pushing the ketch at a nice speed. Lola was having a fine time jumping from mast to mast, something she liked to do when the boat was moving with the sails unfurled. But for some reason she couldn't let go of that last argument they'd had. At one point, she swooped down and grabbed the flashlight from my unsuspecting father-in-law and threw it overboard. Bernard was angry. He went after her, but Lola was too quick. The two yelled at each other as Bernard chased her around the deck. Eventually, just as he was about to grab her, she jumped overboard.

I figured that was it. Lola was gone. I knew she would never make it back onto a moving boat. My heartfelt sadness, tinged with relief, was replaced by disbelief when I saw her tiny head poke up over the stern—soaking wet and triumphant.

We later discussed what we should do with this unpredictable creature. It was a delicate subject. Bernard loved her, but the situation was getting serious. She was getting into everything on the boat, so we couldn't leave her behind when we went to shore. And because she had no papers, we always had to hide her in a shoulder bag when we took her with us. She couldn't be trusted around matches. She had already eaten the teak off one of the lockers under the sink in the galley, and was starting on another.

I suggested taking her to the zoo, but Bernard couldn't do it. We were at a stalemate. It was a big problem with no obvious solution.

Several days later, we were invited to a party at the home of one of my colleagues. We couldn't leave Lola behind. We'd already tried putting her in a bucket suspended from the ceiling, with a net fastened overtop, before going out. While we were gone, she had managed to swing the bucket from side to side and, with a hand stretched through the net, had shredded the curtains covering the portholes in the salon.

So we shoved her into a shoulder bag and took her with us. Our idea was to tie her to a bedpost in the bedroom of our host. However, within minutes of her confinement, she had ripped apart the bedding. Our host was not amused. Lola had gone from a novelty to a liability.

"She has to go," I said.

This time Bernard agreed with me.

The next day, we took her to the Singapore zoo. The zookeeper told us that they generally don't take domesticated monkeys because they can't adjust, but Lola was still young and he thought she might get adopted into the group. We went with her to the monkey house and saw that there were about a dozen monkeys that looked exactly like her.

We felt the adjustment would be easy. But Lola saw it differently. She looked at the fellow members of her species and was terrified. She had no idea what they were. The zookeeper assured us that she would be OK. We told him that we would come back in a few days to see how she was doing.

When we returned a week later, Lola was part of the pack. It was even hard to differentiate her from the others, and she had lost all interest in us.

The last day we saw Lola was hard on Bernard. He'd saved her life, and she had a special place in his heart. As for Lola, although gratitude wasn't high on her list of priorities, it was clear that she had felt something for Bernard. But she was a crab-eating macaque, and as a fish-eating monkey, she had other fish to fry. So did we, and we set sail for Thailand a short while later.

Rita Pomade spent seven years with her husband on a sailing adventure that took them from the China Sea to the Mediterranean. During those years they encountered pirates, scamps, madmen and dreamers. Dropping anchor wherever they pleased and for as long as they wanted, they often found more adventure than they bargained for. This story was adapted from a book that Rita is now writing about their travels.

Willow Tales

She's smarter than you think.

By Jacqui Morrison

I distinctly remember the day we rescued our golden retriever, Willow. She was living with a family who no longer wanted her.

When she came bounding out to greet us she did so with the exhilaration of a puppy, yet it was apparent that she had the maturity of a young adult dog. She had thick golden fur the color of wheat and liquid brown eyes with copper highlights. We also noticed that she had only three legs, and that her left front paw bowed to accommodate her weight. Never in my life have I felt so immediately attached to a dog.

Willow doesn't seem to realize that she's different—or does she? We live in Orillia, Ontario, which overlooks Lake Couchiching, and she loves to retrieve sticks from the lake on hot summer days, just like many other dogs.

She also loves little toys that we buy for her at the dollar store. At first she cuddles with the toys, carrying them around the house in her mouth. But after about three days she'll have gingerly chewed off the right front leg of any toy we've given her. This is the most remarkable thing about Willow.

We call her stuffed toys "babies" and often ask her, "Where's your baby?" She'll come bouncing in with a stuffed animal that is inevitably missing its right front leg. Every time we get her a new toy this is what she does.

I remember retelling the story about Willow and how she defiles her "babies" to a friend's son. I am an animated storyteller who tends to exaggerate my hand gestures when I tell my tales. The poor kid became pale in the face and fixed me with the most horrified look. He said, "She rips the paws off her puppies?"

I guess in my lively description I neglected to mention that the "baby" I was referring to was a stuffed animal. I hope he's not in therapy over the story.

A coworker thought I was fabricating the story of Willow chewing off the right leg of her stuffed toys. On our lunch we went to the dollar store and she helped me pick out a little toy for Willow. Three days later I delivered to my coworker a clear plastic bag with the stuffed animal—minus the right front leg. My coworker is now a believer. She has advised me to get an animal behaviorist to analyze my special dog.

Willow really does not like dark-haired men wearing baseball caps. I suspect her original owner may have hit her because she shows her teeth whenever a dark-haired man with a baseball cap comes to the house. I had to tell a visiting plumber to remove his hat before he came in.

A friend of ours—also with dark hair—once offered to install crown molding in our house. I left a key so that he could let himself inside, then walked to my local coffee shop to have a drink while the work was being done.

A few minutes later I received a call at the coffee shop. It turns out that Willow wouldn't let the man into our home. Once I returned, she no longer barred her teeth at the man.

I had a serious knee injury one summer, which forced me to drive my electric scooter all over town. I didn't want to leave poor Willow at home, so I walked her beside my scooter whenever I went out. A passing motorist nearly hit the curb when he realized that Willow only had three legs and was being "walked" by a woman wearing a cast.

Our local animal shelter organizes an event they call the "Mutt Strut," where pet owners raise pledges for a walk that supports the shelter. There are prizes for pets that can do tricks. For our trick Willow put her left paw on my shoulder in an impromptu hug— which the organizers thought was prize-worthy. She received a Frisbee and a blanket for her efforts. The Frisbee is a perfect toy to throw in the lake and, since it doesn't have legs, she won't alter it.

Willow is aging now. We've had her for about seven years. When she came into our life she resembled an exuberant puppy. Now she can no longer lift her remaining front paw onto my shoulder. Her sight may be failing because she will bark nonstop whenever we have guests, and she does not seem to recognize many people.

Willow, the wonder dog, is a memorable part of our family's history. Her tales will forever be etched in our hearts.

Jacqui Morrison lives in northern Ontario. She is an author, workshop leader, and the Writer in Residence for the Parry Sound Public Library. Her mystery novel Kaitlyn Wolfe, Crown Attorney *won the Gold IPPY award for Best Fiction for Central and Eastern Canada in 2009. Her second novel—*The Vigilante*—was released in 2013. She has also been published in three anthologies and has many magazine articles to her credit. Jacqui adores her golden retriever, Willow, but finds that her two cats are not as fond of the wonder dog. You can visit her at* **www.jacquimorrison.ca***.*

Animal Farm

Growing up in the country ain't for sissies.

By Alan Longworth

School came to an abrupt end for me at age fourteen. I got my education out behind the barn—learning how to milk cows, slop hogs, and spread manure—which in the world of farming is tantamount to a degree. Of course, there were postgraduate courses on sheep shearing, calf castration, and equipment maintenance, not to mention off-the-farm skills that I had to learn, such as dancing and dating etiquette.

So where does my urge to write stories come from? After thinking long and hard about this I have come to the conclusion that it's the result of mild brain damage. My first brain injury occurred when I fell through a rotted loft floor into the cow barn. I have little memory of either the journey down or smashing my head on a cow's water bowl.

However, I do remember waking up with a Fordson-tractor-sized headache. Cow drool was cascading down my cheeks, and I realized that a milk cow was layering my face with long, saliva-covered licks. I have no idea if I tasted good to her; perhaps, since I had appeared from above, she considered me a gift from God. I recall lying there for some time gazing into her big brown eyes, even as a tongue with the texture of a hoof rasp caressed my already dripping face. I can't remember how long I lay there, but I do know that I did not feel any immediate urge to become a writer at that point.

The next and most significant head injury came as a result of having my head crushed under the hoof of a giant Clydesdale horse. My brother George and I—riding in the manure cart behind our horse—were returning to the farmyard for another load of manure. Wishing to relive the wild days of the Roman charioteers, George whipped the Clydesdale into a wild gallop. Suddenly the bit popped off the bridle and out of the horse's mouth. We were out of control as old Bob headed for his home in the stable.

The problem was that stable doors are not constructed to accept manure carts entering. And since the phrase "Houston, we have a problem!" had not yet been invented, George instead yelled, "Jump out and stop him, Alan!"

Being weak-willed and easily led, I leapt from the speeding cart.

Bob turned his head sideways as I grabbed for the bridle. I tripped over his huge front leg and fell down. In his next stride, Bob's hind hoof—the size of a meat platter ringed in iron—tramped on my skull. Following old Bob was the manure cart, its left wheel pushing my already throbbing noggin deep into the soft spring soil. I think I must have slept for a while, for when I could see again, the horse, cart, and George were heading over the horizon with harness chains jangling and George bravely riding the chariot as if to some ancient war. "Don't you dare tell anyone," he told me on threat of retribution. I remember suffering the effects of concussion for better than a week.

There's something about life on the farm that leads to unexpected adventures. Mother bought my brothers and me a nanny goat, perhaps hoping that having a pet might cut down on our misdeeds. Nanny was white in color—a pretty animal with a goatee beard like Lenin and yellow eyes like a Bengal tiger. But Nanny also had the devil inside her. She could get into trouble while we were still asleep.

One of our favorite games with Nanny was to tie a rope around her neck and tie the other end onto the front of one of our bicycles. A few tugs on the rope would send Nanny sprinting forward, giving us a burst of hitherto unknown speed. As often as we tried, we could never train her to run in a straight line. She must have caught on to our antics, because invariably she would take to the high ground or hurtle through a hole in a thorn hedge. Needless to say, we humans could not follow and were unceremoniously ejected from our bikes while Nanny continued running until the wrecked bicycle held her like a ship's anchor. Not surprisingly, being pulled into a thorn hedge caused one's forehead to become the braking system. And since bicycle helmets had not yet been invented, this added to my list of brain injuries.

Like all goats, Nanny liked to survey "her" world from a high perch. We had a lot of stone walls on the farm, from which she spent an inordinate amount of time surveying the world around her with what always looked like a smirk on her face. I now wonder if Nanny's evil mind was plotting the next escapade.

Nanny also loved to stand on top of automobiles. She preferred the roof for its vantage point, but if it was a soft-top she was quite willing to settle for standing on a car's hood. This was always a surefire way to scratch shiny car parts with her cloven hooves.

It always appeared to me that visitors who came to our farm were absent a sense of humor. I recall many salesmen who parked in our yard—coming out of the farmhouse after making a sale—would quickly lose their smile when they saw Nanny sitting on her haunches looking like a gigantic hood ornament. This sometimes resulted in the offended salesman running back to the house screaming profanities at my mother, thereby losing both his reputation as a nice fellow and the opportunity of repeat sales.

A traveling salesman in his hardware van made a monthly stop at all the farms in our area. It had roll-up sides that allowed him to better display his wares. It was the proprietor's custom to open the sides before going to the house to bring mother out to make her purchases. Nanny, who was always aware of the goings-on at the farm, seized the opportunity to go shopping on her own. Seconds after the proprietor had gone to the house to exchange pleasantries with mother and coax her to come out to the van, Nanny was aboard his vehicle searching for edibles; these ranged from wash leathers to bars of fancy soaps and dishcloths. By the time they returned to his vehicle, Nanny had scoffed the value of half of our week's milk check.

Nanny's next escapade turned out to be her last. My father was very ill and was confined to his bed. In those days doctors made house calls. Father's doctor came to see him, and being a regular caller, he came to the little-used front door and left it open as he went to see my father upstairs.

Nanny, eventually becoming bored with leaving tracks all over the doctor's pricy new car, wandered in through the open front door. Her penchant for high places led her onto the big sideboard, where to her delight my mother had placed a large vase of flowers. Chrysanthemums were a new delight when compared to Nanny's normally mundane diet. She tucked in with gusto until my mother came downstairs with the doctor. Nanny knew that she would be in trouble, so she made a leap for the door.

Mother was proud of her sideboard and kept it well waxed and polished. This proved to be challenging for Nanny to negotiate. Her hard hooves skidded on the shiny surface as she tried to gain a foothold. The vase of flowers and other ornaments were hurled around the sitting room by flying hooves.

The doctor reacted like he had been shot and began yelling profanities. Mother reacted with a scream of anger at Nanny, who by now had exited the house and made her way up onto the roof of the doctor's car again.

A heated discussion ensued. In hindsight, I now believe it was an ultimatum. "Either the goat goes, or you can hire your husband a new physician," the doctor told my mother. The next morning Nanny was gone forever.

To ease our disappointment, mother bought us a donkey. We never gave the animal a name; we just referred to it as Donkey. It is my theory that, somehow, Donkey received secret training in bad behavior from Nanny. How this was achieved is not known, but Donkey was just as ornery as Nanny had been.

Sometimes, Donkey would allow us to ride him and pretend that we were cowboys. However, these rides were usually short-lived. When Donkey had tired of unruly boys climbing on him, he developed a number of methods for dislodging us. At other times, Donkey refused to budge, no matter how much we encouraged him.

One fine day, my brother George had taken his turn at bareback riding. As the second eldest boy, it was now my turn. I climbed aboard and held fast to the "handles" (Donkey's ears), but Donkey refused to move. We cajoled him and we encouraged him, but Donkey was adamant: he was not giving his tormentors any more rides that day.

Brother George, always full of ideas, decided to whack Donkey's rump with a big stick. With the speed of a ballistic missile, Donkey set off at a mad gallop as I desperately clung to him. Donkey ran down the farm lane until he had reached a prominent section of thorn hedge. Without hesitation, he turned and shot through the thorn hedge, scraping me off his back like dung from a shoe. Donkey carried on at a gallop to the far side of the meadow, where he began to graze. Bleeding profusely, I walked back to the farmhouse to have mother fill the thorn holes in my face. After subjecting us to several more near-death experiences, he too eventually disappeared in the dark of night.

Mind you, this did not put an end to our desire to ride the range on the back of a fine steed. We next took to pig riding. This requires special skills because of the way pigs run, moving their long backs in a swinging motion. We would mount our chosen steed and release it from a chute, just like at the rodeo. If we could stay on the pig for thirty or forty feet, it was considered a long distance. The experience generally ended with the bareback rider being thrown or wiggled off, and landing unceremoniously facedown in the dirt.

Somehow my brothers and I survived our youth. But I've become convinced that the accumulation of brain injuries is what has caused me to become a writer, a vocation with long hours and virtually no remuneration.

Alan Longworth left school at age fourteen to labor on his family's farm, where he worked until he was twenty-one. After a varied career, he began writing after retirement and has completed seven novels, a book of humor, and several short stories. He received an award from the Noah society for a short story titled "My Animal Friends," and two other awards for his short fiction. He enjoys writing several types of poetry, including "cowboy poetry," which he often performs publicly.

Tit for Tat

There's a little bit of crazy cat lady in all of us.

By Lois Gordon

Calvin was homely, even as a youngster. He was the only kitten who never once evoked coos and cries of joy at his sweet face. Now as an adult, he has an undersized head, oversized eyes, a long striped body, and a crooked tail that points to magnetic north. If Calvin were a painting, he'd be mounted on black velvet and priced for clearance at a parking-lot flea market. As cats go, well, let's just say that I should have named him Edsel.

Now, I don't want you thinking that I'm a cat person, because I'm not. Nor do I aspire to become a cat person. There's simply no return on investment with a cat. Lay down your money and what do you get? Indifference. Puked-up hair balls. Tattered furniture. The Litter Box. A four-legged demon who peers at you through glinting yellow eyes from atop your shredded sheer curtains.

A dog … now that's a pet! Take a German shepherd for a walk in the park and see how many guys notice you. "Nice dog," they'll say, smiling. Would they stop if they saw me walking my cat? I think not.

But I digress.

Calvin and I were brought together by Fate, that hag. He was lurking in the garage of the house I was moving into—abandoned, it seems, by the previous owners, who are apparently much wiser than I am. His pitiful mewing—which had the musical cadence of a Mongolian throat singer—sent me running to the corner store for kibble and milk. He lapped everything up, then tucked himself into the palm of my hand and purred, his undying gratitude apparent in every lick of his sandpaper tongue. No, that's not when I decided to keep him because, in case you weren't paying attention, I'm not a cat person.

Cute? Somewhat. Mine? No. He had to go.

I returned to said corner store and posted a notice: FREE KITTEN TO A GOOD HOME. A week later I came back and scratched out the words "TO A GOOD HOME."

Unfortunately there were no takers.

So I named him Calvin (he was neither clever nor charming enough to be Hobbes) and officially adopted him, which means that I spent three hundred bucks on vet bills and colorful cat toys. "All I can say is you'd better be a good mouser," I warned him as I scooped Cuddles cat litter into a shiny, new plastic bin.

My gentle German shepherd, Hannah, became his surrogate mother. She let the kitty nestle into her warm tummy as she lay on the floor. Calvin searched in vain for a nipple, and when he couldn't find one, he suckled the soft folds of Hannah's belly instead. She licked his head and gently poked him with her big black nose.

In return for her unconditional love, Calvin would spar with her snout, use her as a mattress, tip over her water bowl, and scatter her food across the kitchen floor. His favorite game was to launch himself from hiding spots to catch a ride on Hannah's tail, claws buried deep, an evil gleam in his eyes. He would swing back and forth, back and forth, with the rhythm of Hannah's wagging tail. And Hannah was always too gracious to rid herself of the uninvited passenger by whacking her tail against the wall a few times. How she put up with this demon's ritualistic torture, I'll never understand. If I had been in Hannah's place, I'd have taken my big paw and batted the little mutant into the middle of next week. But then, unlike my dog, I don't particularly like cats.

When Hannah passed away, Calvin and I were devastated. For three weeks his tortured meow threatened to drive my sanity over the edge. Unable to locate an exorcist, I instead made a trip to the local animal shelter and bought Calvin a new friend: a three hundred and fifty dollar pound kitty (fifty bucks for the kitten, three hundred for vet bills and colorful cat toys) whom I named Annie.

OK, I'll admit it. Lying entwined in each other's arms, they looked kind of cute. I began to comprehend their appeal, and that scared the heck out of me. I had nightmares of becoming the neighborhood's middle-aged crazy woman who lived "alone" with nine cats. Because that's how it starts, you know: those innocent, fuzzy faces cast a spell on your cold, cold heart until you have a coven of kitties. I swore it would never happen to me.

Calvin is still with me. He's almost seventeen years old and, like I said, he hasn't improved much with age. He spends most of his days curled up beside Annie, napping. His meow has taken on the cadence of a dying whoopee cushion, and he lets the other cats—yes, I said cats!—groom the parts of his coat he can no longer reach with his tongue. The youngest of my five $350 pound kitties, Cloud, spars with Calvin's nose, wrestles with his tail, and leaps at him from any number of hiding spots.

I just smile. Retribution.

*Lois Gordon is an author and interior designer. Fearing that she would become the crazy spinster lady with nine cats, she married later in life and moved to a hobby farm in southern Ontario, where she lives with her husband and a menagerie of farm animals. Cats are the least of her problems. For more of Lois's humor stories, visit her online at **www.loisgordonwriter.com**.*

The Ostrich

Pride bounceth and pitcheth sideways before a fall.

By Russell Jennings

I felt like a bronc buster at the Calgary Stampede as I desperately clung to the ostrich. It leapt into the air, twisted, turned, and bounced up and down as if it were on a pogo stick. Then, abruptly, the ostrich stopped in its tracks. I pitched sideways, slingshotting into a sloppy quagmire of mud and manure.

I had been on its back for a scant three seconds!

Experiences like this are common in Oudtshoorn, South Africa—which is famous for its ostrich show farms. When I first arrived I could see spectators grouped at a corral, so I dashed over to see what was going on. There were four ostriches milling around an ostrich keeper—a wiry, dark-skinned man who was speaking to the crowd.

"The ostrich has a brain no bigger than its eye," he said. "The plumes of females are dull brown, while those of males are black and white."

The man spoke articulately and his talk was well rehearsed.

"Ostriches are the largest birds in the world, but they can't fly because their wings aren't strong enough to lift their bodies. Males can weigh more than three hundred pounds. Each foot has two toes of varying lengths. The longer one has a sharp nail, and if aggravated, an ostrich can kick with enough force to crack a man's ribs or break a leg."

I chuckled. Who in their right mind would want to aggravate an ostrich?

"These four ostriches are males." He pointed to the four giant birds next to him. "I have ridden each of them. They are tame. Would someone like to ride one?"

I looked at the muddy ground, saturated with the previous night's rain and spattered with white ostrich droppings. The last thing I wanted to do was wallow in it.

The man looked around for a raised hand. "Nobody?"

I'm usually content to let others do the volunteering, but this time no one did. Before I could stop myself I had raised my hand. The next thing I knew I had climbed on top of the corral fence, mounted the ostrich nervously and, within three seconds, had fallen into the slush. I picked myself up amidst the laughs and cheers of the spectators.

I realized my mistake. I should have gripped the bird's wings tighter. I called for another ostrich, hoping it was not aware of my inexperience.

The ostrich keeper picked up his long pole, which had a hook at one end, and stealthily approached another ostrich. He hooked it by the neck and drew the ostrich toward the fence where I was teetering and waiting to mount. There are no such things as saddles for ostriches; bareback is the only style. I lowered myself gently onto its feathered back and took a deep breath.

The ostrich gave a quick start, but the pressure of the keeper's hook against its neck prevented it from leaping away prematurely. I grabbed hold of the shoulders, where the bony wings joined the body, then placed my legs in front of the ostrich's thighs. Lastly,

I tucked my knees under the bird's feathered armpits. I felt snug and secure.

"Are you ready?" the keeper asked.

I hesitated for a moment. "Ready."

When the keeper released the hook from around the bird's neck, the ostrich sprang forward, jumping up and down as if it were on a trampoline. It tried desperately to catapult me into the air by charging towards the corral fence, then stopping just short. Like the previous bird, it was expecting me to rocket over its head and into the muck. But somehow I managed to hold on.

The ostrich jerked its body left and right, desperately trying to free itself from my grip. I clutched its wings ever tighter and pressed my legs against its flanks. I could feel my leg muscles beginning to cramp.

Below me was the slush. I didn't relish another mud bath! As the crazed bird dashed around the compound in circles and tight figure eights, I started to plan my dismount. The spectators were just a blur, but I clearly heard their cheers and laughter.

As the bird leapt up and down, its long thin neck wavered and jerked before my eyes. It was time for me to jump to safety and declare myself the victor.

That's when the ostrich lowered its head. I lurched forward. Before I could regain my balance, I slid—head first—down the long neck and into the slush. I curled myself into a ball and prayed the bird wouldn't kick me.

When I raised my mud-streaked face I saw the ostrich prancing around the corral—declaring itself the winner!

Since Russell's encounter with the ostrich he has limited his mounts to cantankerous camels, lumbering elephants, horses, and the occasional stubborn donkey. Russell met his wife Penny on a blind date in Vancouver. He was en route from Australia, his home country, to South America, via Southeast Asia and Alaska. Since the day they met they have backpacked many thousands of miles and chronicled some of their travels in Around the World in Sandals, *and* Timbuktu, Where are You? *as well as penning the informative* Travel Planner's Weather Guide. *You can find Russell and Penny Jennings at **www.openroadtravels.com**.*

Doggone Dogs

Of course you realize: this means war!

By Donald Dowden

In 1948, which was the era of bicycle delivery boys who carried groceries, meat, and prescription drugs to their customers citywide, my mother volunteered me to fill a part-time position at the Jarvis Grocery, which was a half-block from our home in Brantford, Ontario.

I was nearing my thirteenth birthday and was small for my age. The act of balancing heavy loads on my bike and safely delivering them to our customers was my first challenge, but I quickly got the hang of it and rather enjoyed the experience. The second challenge was more of an occupational hazard: dogs!

Some of the dogs I encountered proved to be formidable foes whenever I passed close to their owners' properties. As my weeks on the job turned into months, I became convinced that dogs in some neighborhoods had banded together to form secret associations, attend clandestine canine meetings, and to map out and coordinate their various attack strategies on me as I went about my delivery rounds.

Most dogs seemed to adhere to an unwritten code of honor. They at least provided adequate notice of their desire to engage you in battle. An honorable dog barked or bayed loudly, or perhaps snarled ferociously, as he advanced upon you at a speed equal to that of the lead tank in a German panzer brigade. There were a few, however, that I regarded as renegades; they seemed to favor a cold, calculated sneak attack on your flank, which you discovered only after your pant-leg had been unceremoniously yanked off a pedal and shredded between the beast's slavering jaws.

I was the first, at least among my contemporaries, to employ the passive defense. If a dog provided his victim—me—with adequate warning, I would immediately pedal furiously, not with any hope of outdistancing the animal, but only to buy sufficient time to perform my next fiendishly clever maneuver. This consisted of placing both feet on my bike's handlebars, which would usually allow me to coast to safety. Unless my attacker was of gargantuan proportions, this raised all essential parts of my anatomy out of harm's way, but was only effective for about a half-block on flat terrain.

This passive defense worked particularly well, however, if a brainless beast chose to attack as I was returning from a delivery to Echo Place. Here I could coast down one of the steep hills on Marlborough or Sheridan Streets, both of which possessed slopes reminiscent of an Olympic bobsled run. If I was willing to risk running the stop sign at the bottom of either hill—and especially if the wind was at my back—it was possible to coast yet another two blocks clear back to the store. No dog, at least in my neighborhood, possessed the conditioning or dedication to pursue me that far.

We were a large and noisy group around the Sunday evening dinner table—the only time I was on hand to eat with the rest of my family. It was often difficult for me, being the youngest, to gain the floor. When I did, I used it to complain loudly about my never-ending problems with those "doggone dogs."

"Donny, why are you always running away from them?" my sister Doreen asked me once.

"What do you want me to do? Stop and do battle with them so that you have one less brother to bug you?"

"No," she patiently continued. "Why don't you try to make friends with them?"

"How do you expect me to do that?" I responded a little peevishly. But not too peevishly, as she was the only one of my eight older siblings who would help me with my grade eight homework.

"Well," she said. "You work in a store. The answer is right under your nose. Why don't you carry little treats in your pockets to give to them?"

Her suggestion stopped me in mid bite. "You may have a point. Let me think about it."

And think about it I did. While I liked the idea, one problem was that doggy treats were still in their infancy at that time, and I didn't have any spare cash to spend on them anyway. But the store I worked at did sell bulk cookies, and broken ones were often available at a very reasonable price. I decided to try it.

"How come you're buying all these old cookies?" asked Charlie, the owner of our tiny corner store. It was Saturday morning and I had just purchased a large bag of broken butter cookies at nineteen cents per pound. He knew that my weakness was for the chocolate marshmallow variety—the ones with strawberry jam spread over the bottom of the biscuit, then heaped with marshmallow and real milk chocolate. I often consumed a dozen of these—at a nickel apiece—to keep body and soul together while making my Saturday morning deliveries.

"Umm. I'm trying to save some money for a new baseball glove," I stammered. I wasn't sure if Charlie would appreciate my efforts to negotiate a peace treaty with the neighborhood canines, especially on his time. So off I went, with unfettered hope in my heart, clutching a wrinkled bag of broken butter cookies against one handlebar.

A mangy, lop-eared spaniel-terrier mix was the first foe I encountered. He spied me approaching along Maitland Street, let me pass, then fell in behind me with long, loping strides. I held my fire until he was within five yards of my bike's rear fender; then I dropped my first piece of cookie. However, my aiming skills were insufficiently developed, and it landed well astern of him.

I prudently sped up, but this complicated the process even more. A steady stream of cookie bits soon stretched out behind him as he worked industriously at detaching my pant leg from the rest of me. After exhausting more than half my ammunition, I kicked him in the slats and he disengaged himself from the fray.

Countless practice sessions followed. I experimented with throwing the cookie bits in front of me, but often Old Blue— my bike—promptly ran over them, reducing the chunks to unrecognizable cookie crumbs. I tried throwing them to the side, but most dogs were either afflicted with poor eyesight or too intent on annihilating me, as my peace offerings continued to fall unnoticed. I next tried "large-caliber ammunition," firing off entire unbroken cookies. I eventually discovered that hitting a dog on the head with a butter cookie usually secured its attention.

Much too soon after my initial success, the word that I was establishing a doggy food bank must have been passed along at the next D.O.G.S. (Dogs on Guard Society) meeting, as I became an overnight favorite of the canine community.

This actually made the situation worse. Inevitably, every street that I rode down now seemed to have three or four frowsy beasts that would come trotting out of their yards, tails wagging, in anticipation of a treat. The friendly approach had obviously developed some shortcomings, not the least of which was the constant drain on my pocketbook.

I considered other proactive solutions, and eventually the answer came to me with a *bang!* The month of May was upon us, and by fortuitous circumstance, Charlie's annual shipment of Victoria Day fireworks had just come through the door. This was a time when real, honest-to-goodness firecrackers—not the pallid, sputtering, repetitious fireworks of today—were available for purchase. Indeed, destructive missiles such as skyrockets were still on the market, and could be placed in empty glass milk bottles and fired randomly into the nighttime sky, occasionally alighting in a neighbor's backyard and burning down his garden shed.

I first broke the truce by employing a string of those minuscule firecrackers, stitched together with a single fuse, which could be dropped surreptitiously scant inches in front of the pursuing dog's nose. A dog has never been born who will tolerate thunder or loud noises of any sort, and this tactic had the remarkable effect of causing every dog to abandon the chase. Indeed, the pursuer-turned-victim usually disgraced itself completely by galloping away in full retreat, with ears and tail at half-mast.

Flushed with success, I moved on to bigger and better things. The larger firecrackers, all of which have long since vanished into obscurity, were now added to my armament. I could wedge one into each of my carrier's handlebar clamps, ready for immediate use at the first sign of a charging dog. I wasn't looking for trouble, but I was ready for it! I began to feel like matinee idol Hopalong Cassidy, with a pistol on each hip. (Whether or not my bicycle, Old Blue, began to imagine it was Hoppy's trusted horse Topper is a matter of conjecture.)

I delivered the coup de grace just before sunset one Saturday afternoon. The chosen victim was Caesar, a large, hairy, brown-and-white beast of uncertain collie parentage who terrorized a sector just two blocks from the store, and who happened to live beside my best friend Bob. From this strategic location it was Caesar's habit—indeed his mission in life—to terrorize me not only when I was attempting to pedal past his stronghold while delivering groceries, but also when I was on my way to and from school, and even to prevent me from visiting Bob.

For the showdown with my ultimate foe I had equipped myself with what can be described as a two-fuse torpedo, a sinister-looking firecracker about the size of a Cuban cigar and with a separate fuse at each end. Upon my approach, Caesar, momentarily surprised and confused by my brash frontal attack, rushed aggressively from between two old juniper bushes in front of his house, confident of winning this skirmish just as easily as he had won the previous dozen. When he had closed to within ten yards, I casually lit both ends of the missile and dropped it in front of his nose, which was careening toward me just ahead of the rest of him.

BANG!

An explosion erupted. Caesar came to a stop so quickly that I could smell the hair burning off his front paws. In his panic, he made a hard right hand turn and ran across the road to what he assumed was a safe vantage point and a place to regroup. What Caesar didn't realize was the first explosion had shot the torpedo clear across the street, where it detonated again just inches from his nether parts. With a mournful wail, the outgunned animal acknowledged defeat and slunk ignominiously down the driveway and into the far reaches of his backyard.

From that day forward, Caesar lost his spirit for the chase. Indeed, whenever he saw me confidently advancing, he would immediately retreat deep into the juniper bushes and cower there silently until I had departed. Following this splendid victory, I turned in my weapons. I had permanently vanquished my longtime foe.

Don Dowden has enjoyed a life-long love affair with words; their sound, their impact, the way some nestle happily side-by-side while others are best kept apart. During his long working career he wrote thousands of words related to advertising, profit plans, presidents' speeches, and more. Since retiring he has produced four short volumes of poetry—one of which is appropriately titled Doggerel and Caterwauling—*and an unpublished memoir* Delivery Boy Days *from which "Doggone Dogs" was extracted and gussied up. He has just completed a mammoth book about more than fifty years of family camping throughout Canada and the United States, in which family dogs Blondie and Misty sometimes experience their own adventures.*

Horsin' Around

A case of Murphy's Law in action.

By Jeannine Philibotte

I'm a longtime fan of horses, so when my friend Robyn decided to take a trip to Maine for the purpose of picking up a rescue horse, she asked me to take care of her stable—twelve horses, including a six-week-old colt named Bogie.

When I arrived at my friend's farm, she gave me some final instructions. "Give each of them a sleeve of hay and one cup of grain," she said. "And if you don't see all twelve of them, ring the cowbell attached to the porch. It always works to bring them in." She also warned me that Bogie wasn't halter broke, which meant that I would have to use hand gestures to direct him to his stall. She also suggested that I keep Chewbacca, their Yorkie, inside the farmhouse, because he loved to chase the horses and had a habit of getting underfoot.

"If you have any questions, here's Brian's cell phone number," she said. Her husband Brian was a veterinarian, and his job was to travel from farm to farm treating his animal patients. "He'll be doing rounds at some of the other farms close by, so if you run into any problems feel free to give him a call."

"Everything will be fine," I assured her. "Go and have some fun."

Shortly after Robyn had left, I thought about the fun day ahead of me as I made my way toward the barn. I loaded hay and grain onto a cart—whistling as I went—before I noticed that five of the horses were not in sight. I decided it would be prudent to go back to the porch and ring the cowbell.

The cowbell must not have been used for some time, because when I rang it a swarm of hornets came buzzing out of the bottom. They had built a nest inside the bell, and having been disturbed by an interloper, were keen to drive her off. I ran toward the front door screaming, but not before I'd been stung on my hands several times. As I had withdrawn my hand, I had also whacked it on the deck railing, and it now sported an open wound.

Once inside, I ran cold water over my swollen fingers, which made them feel marginally better. One of my hands was close to twice its normal size, so I wrapped it in a pink towel and secured it with electrical tape.

When I went back into the living area I noticed that the front door was wide open and the dog was missing. Had I really left it open when I came inside to treat my wounds?

I ran outside, careful to keep my swollen, pink-towelled hand in the air so as to prevent more swelling. This was how I neglected to see the mud puddle on the pathway. It turned out to be a rather deep mud puddle, as one of my boots immediately got stuck. However, the momentum of my body kept me barreling forward.

Any idea what happens in such a scenario?

That's right. My foot came out of the boot and I fell face-first into the muck.

I picked myself up and looked accusingly at my boot. I walked over and gave it a tug, but it was stuck and wouldn't budge. I pulled harder. Still nothing. Eventually I put my entire weight behind it and, after several seconds of straining, managed to break the suction with an impressive *slurp!* The bad news? It put me off balance just enough so that I fell backward into the mud puddle again.

When I looked over, I could see the horses neighing and prancing beside the fence. Were they laughing at me, or just hungry? I chose to believe the latter.

I hopped over to the cart on one foot—which must have looked ridiculous, even to the horses—and put my boot back on. Then I distributed their meal.

I found a relatively dry spot on the grass, and with my pink-toweled hand still in the air, I cleaned myself up as best I could. I removed both boots in turn and whacked them against a post to get as much mud off as possible.

That's when I noticed my friend's dog Chewbacca, who was latched onto a mare's tail and having the ride of his life.

I jumped up and leapt over another mud puddle … right onto the prongs of a pitchfork. Although the prongs did not cut through the bottom of my boot, I landed with enough force to cause the handle to swing up and smack me in the face.

I felt like I was living a movie called *The One Stooge*. Except the slapstick routine was not fake.

A black eye was already forming by the time I reached the mare and managed to detach the dog from its tail. I secured him in the house again and decided to take a short break, with an icepack for my right eye and a well-deserved glass of lemonade. For the next two hours I sat on the porch, grateful that my ordeal was finally over. How could so many things go wrong in a single day? The ranching lifestyle was not for sissies!

Later that afternoon, I could hear the rumble of thunder reverberating in the distance. Dark clouds started to form in the sky. I did not want the horses to be out in a storm, so I hurried to put them back in their stalls. I saved the colt for last, as I knew he would need special instructions.

With the other horses safely secured in the barn, I approached Bogie so that I could give him hand gestures. To my surprise, this caused him to run in the opposite direction. I chased after him, hopping awkwardly across the field to avoid mud puddles with my pink-toweled hand flailing in the air.

Just then I heard a mysterious flapping sound. I looked up to see a pigeon dropping from the sky to land on my head. What the...? That's when I realized it was Peetie, the tame pigeon that Robyn and Brian kept on their back porch.

Just then, thunder rolled across the sky. I frantically tried to shoo Peetie off my head, but the harder I tried the tighter he held on. The pigeon must have been frightened by the approaching storm, and had come to the nearest person for comfort. It felt like this comedy act went on for hours—but it was five minutes at the most.

That's when I noticed a vehicle pulling into the farmyard. It was Robyn's husband Brian, back from doing his rounds as a farm vet. To say that he was surprised to find me with Peetie the pigeon on my head, and running around the horse pasture flapping my pink-toweled hand in the air, is an understatement.

"Do you need any help?" he shouted.

I stopped dead in my tracks and hollered: "Does it *look* like I need help?!"

When he approached me, I could see that he was having

trouble containing his laughter. He later told me that when I spoke to him my head was bobbing up and down, and Peetie the pigeon was bobbing up and down with it.

He gently removed Peetie from my head and sent him on his way.

He then explained that the colt was afraid of bright colors, so waving the pink towel in the air was scaring him. He made some clicking noises with his mouth and soon the colt was by his side; with a single hand gesture Bogie was securely in his stall.

I stood there in amazement. My hair was a rat's nest and my eye a lovely shade of purple, which—on the bright side—closely resembled the color of the towel on my hand.

"I think I'll leave now," I said, not really sure what to say.

"Thanks for your help," said Brian. And to his credit, he did his best to keep a straight face as I drove from the farmyard.

"So how was your fun day with the horses?" my husband Ron asked when I opened the front door.

I muttered something under my breath as I hobbled inside and slammed it shut.

Ron stared at me inquiringly. "What's that pink thing on your hand?"

Jeannine Philibotte is a retired nurse who has had several essays published on the long-running This I Believe *website, and a short story on **www.e-stories.org**. With her "It's never too late" philosophy, she recently learned to ride horses. She and her husband Ron have been married for forty-seven years.*

Lamb of God

You want me to do what?

By Philip Torrens

It had been a rough voyage, and the ice now blocking my kayak's course seemed like the last straw.

Two of us had left from Toronto nearly three weeks earlier, madly keen to paddle to Montreal. "Madly" seemed the apt word in retrospect: we had set out in mid-March, while the shores of Lake Ontario were still white with snow. We'd been stormbound for days at a time, had been forced to attempt siege-like landings on ice-covered shores, and had even had a tent destroyed in a sleety storm.

A week into the trip, my companion, plagued by back and hand ailments, had been forced to call it quits. Since then, I'd pressed on alone. To be sure, I'd enjoyed some good moments—exhilarating launches where I simply tobogganed in my loaded kayak down frozen embankments into the water, and a trance-like hour kayaking through water so calm that the approaching headland seemed suspended in space and time.

I'd also had bad moments. There was a near-fatal "shortcut" across the mouth of a wide bay that had taken me out of the land's lee, from where I had barely managed to claw back to shore through the teeth of the wind. There were evenings when I landed so sheathed in ice that I had to hammer both my life jacket and my boat's hatch covers with my paddle before they could be removed.

That morning, I'd broken camp and set out, cheered by the calm, sunny weather, and by the prospect of landing in Kingston in the next day or two. I'd decided to cut the trip short at Kingston for one primary reason. If paddling a large, icy lake was foolish, paddling the St. Lawrence—a large ice-choked river—would have been lunacy.

By midafternoon, I'd reached the channel between the mainland and Amherst Island, which sprawled long and low on my right. To my surprise and dismay, the channel was blocked by ice. I'd encountered lots of large ice chunks on previous days, but they'd been loosely scattered and easy to work through. Here, they were tightly packed, stacked together by the prevailing wind, or perhaps by the outflow to the nearby St. Lawrence. I followed the only lead, which zigzagged through the pack like a lightning bolt before coming to a dead end two kilometers later. With the short afternoon wearing on, I was increasingly nervous about the ice suddenly shifting and trapping me. Discouraged, I backtracked to the island.

Once beached, I noticed a small farmhouse through the trees. I trudged up to the house to ask for water and to inquire about camping on their land. I was greeted with true charity by the husband, Ian, and was offered not only water, but supper and a bed for the night. After a good home-cooked meal, I drifted off to sleep beneath a comforter in a brass-framed bed. I was warm and my stomach was full, so it didn't take long.

The next day the ice looked as treacherous as it had the day before, but my hosts seemed happy to let me stay. Determined to earn at least part of my keep, I followed Ian out to the barn to see how I might be of use. Our first task was to break bales of straw to scatter on the floor—it was lambing season and the ewes needed fresh bedding.

As a city kid, I hadn't seen a live birth before, so I watched in fascination. In contrast to the *Sturm und Drang* that television had conditioned me to expect, what was striking about the ewes was their complete equanimity toward—indeed, indifference to—the miracle of birth. They stood placidly, munching on food, while baby dropped out the stern. Sometimes, the lamb would begin to emerge misaligned, so Ian would have to shove it back from whence it came and rearrange it to avoid damage to mother and child.

Once, as he was thus engaged, a second "misbirth" started a meter away. Ian waved me over, and thrust me into the breach, as it were. Nervous as I was—an intern performing his first examination—I was soon elbow-deep in my endeavor. I glanced anxiously toward the mother-to-be's face to see if I was hurting her. She was not missing a beat—or rather, a bite. (However, based on this experience, whenever I've jocularly suggested to human females that they're making a mountain out of a molehill regarding the birth process, the notion has been coldly received at best.)

A few moments after I withdrew my arm, the lamb emerged safely into the world. I watched with a pleased and proprietary air as she struggled to stand, wobbling like a bagpipe on puppet strings.

It was then that the epiphany struck.

"The Lord is my Shepherd..." Even to people like me, not raised in a Christian household, these words are familiar. So familiar, we rarely give them much thought. They invoke a pleasantly pastoral image, often depicted in prayer-book pictures or stained-glass windows. But now, with the force of revelation in my arms, my understanding of these words leapt from abstract to literal. It was an emotional experience.

As I cradled the helpless lamb, I understood how powerful the shepherd metaphor would have been to the actual shepherds of Biblical times. They would have believed that God was to them as they were to their flocks: infinitely wiser and more powerful, and, as a result, capable of infinite compassion. They would have understood the introduction to the 23rd Psalm in a way unattainable to modern urban dwellers, Christian or not. I sat there, rocking the lamb, suffused in a warm glow, richer in my head and in my heart for the experience.

It is in search of moments like these that I travel. By definition, you cannot know what you do not know, so you cannot seek such moments directly. You can only set the stage and prepare your mind by sweeping aside, however temporarily, ordinary concerns. I find the best way to do this is to travel, preferably under my own power. A single instant of such insight is worth weeks of what some might consider deprivation and hardship.

Now if this was a fictional tale, after birthing the lamb I would have immediately, and permanently, become a true believer. But it's a real-life story. I was, and still am, an agnostic—not prepared to embrace a belief merely because it is vastly appealing. Intellectual honesty requires proof, not mere faith. That same intellectual honesty also requires me to acknowledge the impossibility of proving that God is not real, which is why I am agnostic rather than an atheist.

Still, while I may not believe in a divine being, I now understand the belief better and why people believe it. Perhaps, not to sound arrogant, I even understand one aspect of that belief better than some believers themselves. And that's a lot to have learned from a lamb.

Though the events of this story happened many years ago, Philip's passion for paddling continues unabated. He works for a major outdoor retailer while penning freelance articles about his many adventures on the side. He thinks of this trip fondly every time he eats roast lamb.

The Basement Visitor

I should have listened to the cat.

By Leslie Bamford

I've always had a love/hate relationship with basements. I love the extra space that a finished basement provides. I love the recreation room with the big TV, comfy futon, electric piano, and cozy gas fireplace. But I hate the dark, dirty corners of the laundry room, the unfinished concrete floors, the dampness, and the spiders. I hate the dusty furnace room and the leaky cold room under the front porch.

My husband is the adventurer in our family. This summer he turned into Captain Bob of Chesapeake Bay and left me to my own devices while he took a sailing course. I had plans of a non-adventurous variety. I was going to write every day, go to the gym, and work in the garden. But no sooner was he out the door than I heard the basement calling. When I was gardening, I found myself thinking about the mess down there. When I was watching the Stanley Cup finals, I could feel vibes from the dark basement corners haunting me. I began to think about mucking out the cold room, a place I detest, and throwing away what we hadn't used in years. I would even brace myself and sweep the spider carcasses away.

Bob would have told me it was symbolic: that my subconscious was calling, that my psychological basement was crying out for inner attention. Thoughts like these made me determined to resist. I resolved to have nothing to do with the basement while he was gone.

Until I had no choice.

It all started with our cat Blackberry. The day after Bob left, the cat had his breakfast as usual and then disappeared. Now, Blackberry is an animal that follows a routine like someone in the Pentagon: he never wavers from it. He lies in the same places at the same times every day. Always. When I couldn't find him, I knew something was wrong. I searched the house and found him in the laundry room, lying on the runner between his litter box and the washer/dryer. I had never seen him lying there before.

"What's up, buddy?" I asked, stroking his silky fur. "Are you sick? Do you need to stay close to your box?"

No answer except for a purr. It occurred to me that sick cats don't usually purr.

"Do you miss Bob?" Before leaving on his sailing course, Bob had been camped out in the laundry room studying navigational charts at his father's antique drafting desk, wearing a toque to keep warm despite the fact that it was May. Whenever I came home from work and I found him there, I would tell myself that other women had husbands who did this. Blackberry sometimes kept him company.

That must be it. The cat was making a statement. I looked forward to telling Bob how much Blackberry was missing him.

I carried Blackberry back upstairs.

He went back downstairs and lay on the runner. I decided to leave him there.

Later in the morning, he finally came upstairs again. "Want to go out?" I asked, hoping to cheer him up. I found his harness and leash and put them on him. We went outside and Blackberry pulled me over to a crack in the driveway, the place where he likes to lie down between the car and the house.

Blackberry stood at attention, ears pricked; his face was alert and his yellow eyes were big and round. After a minute he looked up and stared at a dryer vent that was attached to the side of our house. I followed his gaze with my eyes, wondering why it had caught his attention.

Then I heard it: a flapping noise.

So much for the "grieving cat" theory. There was a critter in the dryer vent and Blackberry had known it all along. That's why he'd been lying in the laundry room. He'd been trying to convey to me that there was a problem. I just misread the message.

I stood in my driveway digesting the fact that there was a creature in my basement and I had to rescue it. I looked longingly at the sunshine, the patio with the chairs set out, the umbrella, and my book lying on the table where I had planned to vegetate for the afternoon. I picked up Blackberry and went back into the house.

My first task was taking the ductwork apart. This required squeezing in behind the washing machine in a space that is too small for my bulk, and squatting down to remove duct tape that has been holding the ductwork together for twenty-four years. The space behind the appliances was my worst nightmare of hideous basement spaces; it was filled with dust and spider webs and dead insects of various sorts. I cringed as I worked, quickly discovering that duct tape is wonderful stuff except when you want to take it off. When it's that old, the tape comes off but the glue part stays on. Getting the ductwork apart required chiseling away the glue with a pair of Cutco sewing scissors—no doubt rendering them useless for cutting anything ever again. All the while, I wondered what kind of creature was inside. I figured it had to be a bird. Or maybe a bat.

Working in such a small space, my back began to hurt, and I was soon covered with dust and grime. I finally wrestled the ductwork apart just enough to look through the vents and realize there was nothing in there. I knew what I had heard, though, and with Blackberry as my witness, I knew I had not imagined it. I theorized that the creature must have been so scared when I began banging around on the vent that it had squeezed itself back out the top. To make sure, I stood and listened for a long time. There wasn't a sound. Relieved, I put the ductwork back together, painstakingly replacing the ancient duct tape with shiny, new silver tape from Bob's workroom. I stood back, pleased with my work. The garden and my book awaited.

Then I heard it again: flapping!

I groaned, grabbed the almost useless scissors, and began to remove the new duct tape. This time I took all the ductwork pieces outside the house and looked through them to make sure something wasn't clinging to the walls.

There was nothing.

OK, this time I was not going to be fooled. There was only one place the creature could be hiding: inside the dryer.

I went back downstairs and stood watching the back of the dryer. As if on cue, a head poked out.

Not a bird. Not a bat.

A chipmunk.

It emerged from the dryer and raced past me through the laundry room and into the recreation room. I ran behind, hoping that Blackberry was still asleep upstairs where he was napping, having finally given up his chipmunk vigil. He was. This was a good thing, because chipmunks are his favorite prey. Not that he has ever caught one since coming to live with us six years ago.

I ran after the chipmunk, chasing it from room to room, but it proved to be faster than a 63-year-old human with trifocals. Catching this little guy was going to require some serious intelligence. An advertisement for a new reality TV show ran through my head:

ARE YOU SMARTER THAN A CHIPMUNK?

I grabbed a blanket from one of the chairs and threw it on the chipmunk, then tried to scoop it up. But it managed to wiggle free as I gathered up the corners. This only made it run faster. It tried to run up the stairs, but fell off the first step. Then it ran back into the laundry room and back inside the dryer.

I couldn't believe it. Why had it not occurred to me to block the hole with a towel after it had come out? It now seemed obvious that a hysterical chipmunk, racing all around our dark basement, would eventually find its way back to where it started—a place it felt somewhat safe.

It seems that I had a lot to learn about chipmunks.

I decided that I would have to reach into the dryer and drag the little guy out. Then I remembered that chipmunks bite. My sister told me. She did research on chipmunks for her Ph.D. by putting radio collars on them and following them from woodlot to woodlot. So I knew that gloves would be required. I found some oven mitts, the ones made of that stuff astronauts use that won't burn even if placed in a flaming barbecue. I squeezed back behind the dryer and tried to reach in. The mitt was too bulky: I couldn't squeeze my hand inside.

I put them aside and found some rubber gloves instead. I reached in. Nothing. I reached farther. Nothing. I reached my entire forearm into the dryer and couldn't find him. Wherever he was, I couldn't reach that far.

I got a dish cleaning brush, and while still wearing the glove, I reached in with the brush turned backwards and poked as far back as I could. I felt something soft and squishy. I poked again. Nothing.

Clearly this approach was not going to work. What about luring it out with peanuts?

I went into the cold room, ignoring the mess, and dug out a small plastic wastebasket. I went out to the garden shed and got a handful of peanuts from the bird feeder. I returned to the basement and tilted the wastebasket on its side in front of the opening at the back of the dryer, leaving a small space so that I could see if the little guy came out.

I had a plan. When he came out of the dryer and into the pail, I planned to stuff a blanket on top, run upstairs, and let him out.

But nothing happened. I stood beside the dryer for ten minutes, sweating and silently willing the chipmunk to come out. He didn't.

What to do? Who do you call about a chipmunk in your dryer? 9-1-1? Ghostbusters? How about an appliance store?

I ran upstairs, stepping over Blackberry—who was still sleeping soundly at the top of the steps—and dialed our appliance store, Metro Karges.

"Hello, can I help you?"

"I need to know how to take the back of my dryer off," I blurted out. "It's a Maytag, about ten years old. I can't figure out how to take it off."

"Why do you want to take it off?"

"There's a chipmunk inside."

Dead silence.

"Hello? Are you still there?"

"Did you say 'chipmunk,' lady?"

"Yes. You know—those little rodents with black and white stripes?"

"Hang on, lady, I'll ask the guys in the back."

I could have sworn I heard a suppressed chuckle. Then I was on hold.

At that moment, my capturing plan unfolded. The chipmunk poked his head out of the dryer again and, lo and behold, he jumped into the wastebasket. I dropped the phone, squeezed behind the washing machine as fast as I could, bashing my knee on the way, and tipped up the pail. Then I stuffed the blanket on top of the chipmunk and started backing out of the tiny space. The chipmunk tried to wiggle out of the wastebasket, but I stuffed the blanket down as hard as I could and ran up the stairs and out onto the driveway. I took the blanket out of the basket and watched as the chipmunk ran off into the garden, apparently unscathed. I could see that it was a healthy looking specimen, actually a bit on the chunky side—a pregnant female perhaps, looking for a place to have her babies? I'll never know for sure. Thankfully, she didn't have them in our dryer.

Then I remembered the phone. I ran back downstairs and picked it up.

"Lady, where did you go?" asked the appliance guy.

"I was saving the chipmunk. I had to drop the phone."

"Did you?"

"What do you mean?"

"Did you save the chipmunk?"

"Yes. I lured it out with peanuts and got a blanket and…"

"Good work, lady. I'll tell the guys in the back." I detected another snort as he hung up.

Feeling proud, I put the ductwork back together with yet more duct tape. Then I fixed the loose flap on the outside of the vent, the one that had enticed the creature down the rabbit hole in the first place, and poured myself a glass of wine. So what if it was only 4:00 p.m.? I figured I deserved it. As I sat on the patio sipping my Zinfandel, I thought about the basement and the chipmunk and what Bob would say.

The universe had spoken: clearly, it was time for me to face my psychological basement and tidy up some of the cobwebs that were haunting me. I had been running around frantically like that chipmunk—from room to room in my psyche—for far too long without any direction or plan. It was time to rescue that part of myself and set it free.

After thinking about it (while having more wine) I felt a shift inside. Maybe there was something to this symbolic stuff after all.

The next day I mucked out the cold room, vacuumed the floor, cleaned the grimy shelves, and took several bags of unnecessary items to Value Village. I vacuumed and dusted the entire basement, including that cramped space behind the washer/dryer. Then I went upstairs and continued to clean and tidy. I was a woman on a mission: there was no stopping me. Whenever I got tired, I reminded myself that I was a woman of intelligence, smarter than a chipmunk and capable of rescue missions beyond the imagination of appliance-store salesmen.

Who says Bob is the only adventurer in our family?

Leslie Bamford is a native of Montreal who now lives in Waterloo County, Ontario. She often fits her writing in around vacations with her husband, most of which are outside her comfort zone. Because of him she once found herself at the helm of a 34-foot sailboat in a storm, despite her aversion to drowning. During another summer he dragged her to the top of the highest peak in Vermont, despite her fear of heights. The following year he made her crawl through pitch-black caves in Kentucky, despite her fear of tight spaces. This year she discovered that she could have adventures of her own while staying at home. She is very proud of this.

Plato

Small in stature, but with a larger-than-life personality.

By Irene Davis

Plato was a miniature schnauzer. He was gray and white, with floppy ears and a short stub of a tail that wagged fiercely whenever he was excited. It especially wagged when any of his favorite people came through the door, when he was gnawing on a chew toy, and of course when it was time to go for a walk.

He was a cuddly little thing who loved to curl up on my stomach and go to sleep.

Plato was originally my daughter's dog, but shortly after bringing him home she took off for Sydney, Australia. She had intended to stay for six months, but stayed for two years instead. Needless to say, when Plato saw her after she returned he went nuts. He pinned her down in an armchair and alternately licked her face and cuddled in under her chin, his stub of a tail whirring madly. He followed her everywhere. He even slept with her.

Nevertheless, in her absence, he had decided that he was *our* dog. When my daughter married the Australian she had imported and moved out, Plato stayed with us.

I remember the time we went on vacation for two weeks and left Plato with them. When we came back, Plato seemed happy at their house and wanted to stay. But when we were leaving, Plato ran to the door and stood there staring up at us. His whole body was quivering, as if to say, "You're not leaving without me, are you?"

Of course we took him home.

Plato was also smart. His favorite toy was his ball. He enjoyed gripping it with his teeth while one of us tried to pull it out of his mouth. When he accidentally dropped it down the radiator vent one day he headed for the basement and stood on-point in the furnace room, staring up at the pipe leading to the radiator, where his nose told him the ball was hiding. The plaintive look on his face seemed to say, "It's right there. You can get it."

"Sorry, Plato. I can't get it," I said. He finally accepted that the ball was gone, but he never did forget it. Though he played happily with his new ball, it never acquired the beloved status of the one in that pipe. Many times we would find him standing beneath the pipe and staring up wistfully.

Walks were his glory. He would fetch his leash and wait patiently while I put it on. Once we were on our way, he would trot proudly along surveying the world that he owned, nose to the ground, sniffing out all those who had traveled before. Every tree, every bush, and every blade of grass received his blessing.

One day we were ambling along (correction: I was ambling along), while Plato was exploring behind me thanks to his long leash. I suddenly realized that cars passing me were slowing down, and the people in them were looking at me and laughing. I turned to see what was so funny, and found that I was dragging an empty leash. Plato was running frantically after me, his legs pumping rapidly. I have no idea how he managed to slip the leash, but then as dogs go he wasn't very big. I realized he must love us, since he could have easily taken off for exotic locations far away.

When he wasn't walking outside, Plato insisted on surveying his world from a perch on the back of an upholstered chair that stood in front of our living room window. He would sit with his bottom firmly planted—on full alert—and would bounce and bark excitedly if someone he felt shouldn't be there ventured onto *his* street.

That chair developed a divot on its back, along with a frayed surface that would periodically shed stuffing. But it would have been pointless to buy new furniture.

I was sitting in that chair one evening talking to a visitor—the chair Plato considered to be his throne. During our conversation I noticed vaguely that Plato was staring up at me from the middle of the room, his body on-point. But I was involved in the conversation and wasn't paying close attention. Plato turned and went to the front door, the one leading outside. That was his signal that he wanted to go out, and my cue to attach the long, sturdy leash to his collar and let him go. I got up and went to the door; Plato zoomed past me, scooted up the chair and settled on his perch.

I stared at him in astonishment. "You little sneak!" I said to him.

He tossed his head, and with a haughty look on his face turned toward the window to survey his world.

Irene Davis has written feature articles, profiles, and essays for an eclectic assortment of magazines and newspapers, and in 2006 she was awarded the Peter Gzowski Literacy Award of Merit for an essay in The Globe and Mail, *which featured anecdotes about her experience as a volunteer tutor in an adult literacy program. She edited and contributed to* Prose To Go: Tales From A Private List, *an anthology of personal essays by Canadian writers. A diehard word nerd, she developed and currently teaches an online grammar course focusing on common problems. Irene sees Plato duplicates everywhere she goes in her hometown of Toronto, and is quite certain a dog that smart has managed to reincarnate himself at least once.*

Drake and the Ducks

Birds of a feather stick together.

By Janice Sabulsky

"Ducks! Baby ducks!" said the breathless voice on the other end of the telephone.

I held the receiver a couple of inches away from my ear and asked, "Sharon, is that you?"

Without acknowledging my question, Sharon continued her tirade. "I think a cat must have got the mother. I'm following them all over the place. I'll call you later."

The one-way conversation ended abruptly. On my scale of unusual occurrences, this was not even on my radar. I poured myself a cup of coffee and surveyed my rescue sanctuary. The doves were cooing softly and the canaries were taking their first bath of the day. The new cockatiel seemed to be settling in with the others. Life was good.

I guess a little background is in order. I live with my husband Leo in Chetwynd, British Columbia, and am known locally as the "Bird Lady." Sometimes people use the word "crazy" in front of that title.

My love affair with birds started innocently enough when I took home a partly paralyzed diamond dove from the local pet store. I built handicapped steps for it so that it could access its perch, and over the next year I began taking other birds from the pet store that were sick or injured. Word got out that I would take injured birds and soon there was a steady stream of them arriving on my doorstep from people who didn't want them anymore.

Sharon was often my "adoption broker." Sometimes people brought their birds over to my house to look after when they went on vacation and never bothered to pick them up again. At any given time I might have seventy or eighty birds in my house—which I now call Simon House, after the first diamond dove I rescued.

It does get a bit noisy in the summer when the sun comes up at 3:30 a.m., but that's why blinds were invented. Some of the birds also harass my husband and our dog Romeo. They've become experts at sounding like the fire pager (my husband is the fire chief) and when it goes off there are several dozen birds that can mimic the sound. It's absolute chaos.

One of the birds has also learned to mimic my husband's voice and sometimes calls out, "Romeo! Romeo!" Our dog runs around in circles, barking and searching for my husband who may or may not be at home at the time.

Back to the story of the ducks. Late in the afternoon, the phone rang again. "You gotta come to Mike's place. You know where Mike the plumber lives, right?" *Click*. One of these days she's going to get a wrong number. Would she even realize it?

I arrived at the property to see three people crouching on the ground as if preparing for a missile attack.

"So," I asked, "what are we looking for?"

As I spoke, they bolted upright and started shouting. I saw a fluffy ball supported by two legs dash under a pickup truck.

"Baby ducks," said Sharon. "Remember?"

I could tell by her tone that she had stopped just short of adding "Duh!" to her answer. I was somewhat grateful for that.

Over the next thirty minutes, the four of us chased, herded, and collected five fuzzy ducklings and put them into a plastic critter keeper.

"I've been following them all day," said Sharon. "There's no sign of the mother. It's getting dark and I'm scared a cat will get them. Here you go."

In one smooth motion, she thrust the box into my hands and turned quickly in the direction of her house. I watched her retreat, her skirt fluttering around her legs and her sandals slapping on her heels.

I turned to speak to the others. They had also vanished.

I looked suspiciously in the direction of Mike's house. I could picture Mike and his friend hiding behind the couch, motioning each other to keep quiet.

At home, I found one of the many birdcages I had stored in the garage, hastily grabbed a water tin, and picked fresh grass for bedding. I placed the ducks in the cage, set the cage on the deck, and studied the ducklings. They were far from ugly. Indeed, they were beautiful!

But that feeling of elation quickly evaporated as the first wave of panic hit me. What could I feed them? My only information on ducks involved a Maggie Muggins story my mother had read to me years before. The duck was named Cornmeal Katie.

Seizing on that one word—cornmeal—I mixed up some cornmeal mash and put it into the cage. The ducks ignored it completely and snuggled in the opposite corner.

The next morning, I rushed out onto the deck to check on my new adoptees. The water bowl was turned over. The cornmeal mash had dried and was sticking to their feathers. They looked like tiny Sputniks with irregular yellow balls protruding from their backsides.

Perhaps a large bowl of water would help them feel more at home—or at least get rid of the Sputnik effect. I emptied the big silver bowl that contained the dog's water, cleaned it, and refilled it with warm water. As I reached to place the first duckling into the water, Romeo appeared at my elbow with an accusatory glare. Ignoring him, I quickly placed the ducks into the bowl.

Just as I was about to congratulate myself for my act of genius, I realized that something was very wrong. The sounds coming from the bowl resembled liquid being mixed in a blender. The ducks hated being in the water, and their tiny feet were turning like eggbeaters! I quickly pulled them out and dried them with a tea towel.

Later that morning I returned from the local feed store clutching a bag of chick starter. I rigged up a wire to secure the water tin to the side on the cage. One duck bustled up to the feed dish, dove in, and started eating the food. The others followed shortly thereafter. I felt triumphant.

Over the next few days they continued to rush around the cage and jump in and out of the water dish. I watched them snuggle with each other and I stroked their soft down coats with my fingers. They were absolutely beautiful.

It soon became apparent that one of the ducks was the leader. When the brood slept, he was always awake, keeping watch. He always tested the water and took the first bite of food before the rest joined in. I decided to name him Drake.

Near the end of the first week I found one of the ducklings huddled in the far corner of the cage. His head was down and his eyes were only partially open. A swell of panic rose in my chest. Maybe the food I'd been giving them was no good after all. Did the misguided bath I gave them cause pneumonia? I carefully put the ailing duck back with the others. I reasoned that they would keep him warm and comfort him.

When I returned home several hours later, I found the little guy back in the corner, barely breathing. I wrapped him up in a washcloth, dribbled some water into his bill and held him close to my chest. I knew what was coming. More than anything, I hated feeling powerless. He gave a little shudder and went limp. I placed him in a shoebox and stared anxiously at the other four.

When I woke the next morning I realized that something strange had happened overnight: the cage had shrunk to half its original size. The ducks could barely turn around without hitting the sides. It was time for an upgrade. I enlisted the help of my son, who rushed over with a large rabbit cage.

I placed a wide, shallow flowerpot into the cage as a water container. Within minutes, the ducklings had tipped it over. I was starting to feel like the parent of an unpredictable adolescent.

Later, I returned to the cage and found the ducks curled up and sleeping inside the flowerpot, basking in the warm sunlight. Drake was looking around like a watchful sentinel. His brown eyes looked at me steadily. He probably thinks I'm pathetic, I thought. These ducklings are thriving in spite of my efforts.

It wasn't long before the rabbit cage became cramped. I dragged out an old vinyl playpen from the garage, put it on the deck, and set the dog's water bowl into the depression. Victory was mine—I had created an enclosure with a built-in pool.

Romeo hung his long ears over the edge of the playpen. Drake lunged at him and he retreated with his head buried under a chair cushion.

Within two weeks, the playpen became stretched to the limit. The ducks were growing and becoming upwardly mobile. Their downy covering was being replaced by beautiful, sleek feathers. Cleaning the enclosure was also becoming more of a problem. What had previously been accomplished with paper towel now required a small shovel.

For the next phase of the housing crisis, I enlisted the help of my husband. He lit his pipe, walked away muttering, and returned within minutes with a huge wooden playpen. We carried the ducks onto the lawn, flipped the playpen upside down, put it over them, and watched them explore the soft grass.

Later that night, as the sun was setting, I sat in a lawn chair enjoying their company. It was then that I realized I was no longer their protector. I had become their captor.

Several days later—and eleven weeks after I had first taken the ducklings home—my husband and I crammed them into the old rabbit cage and headed for a pond. I held the cage on my lap as we drove and felt a tear sliding down my cheek. Was I about to make the biggest mistake of my life? Would they survive and know what to do without having their food dish filled all day long? Would the other ducks in the lake bully them?

We walked to the edge of the pond and set the cage down. Neither of us wanted to make the first move. Finally, I opened the cage and stepped back.

Nothing happened.

Just as I was beginning to feel that familiar sensation of panic, Drake exited the cage and walked boldly to the edge of the water. He flew forward and alighted on the pond's surface, skating across the water like a skipping stone.

In unison, the others followed Drake's lead. I watched them with a familiar sense of joy and sadness. Like children, they had never really been ours to keep.

A week later we returned to the pond. I called and called for the ducks. At the far end of the lake we finally spotted Drake, marching proudly, the other three following behind him with an air of unbridled confidence.

Not wanting to relinquish the serenity of the pond, we sat on a couple of stumps and enjoyed the atmosphere. As I got up to leave, I caught a movement from the corner of my eye. I found myself staring into Drake's familiar, soft brown eyes. He remained beside me, looking at the others who were out in the pond, and then looked back at me. Then he walked back to edge of the pond and slipped gracefully into the water. Life was good for all of us.

Janice Sabulsky has been taking birds into her home for almost a decade. A few years ago she began taking pictures of her birds and this led to the creation of five children's books, which include photos and stories about her flock. "Drake and the Ducks" was initially written as a children's book so that she could share the story of the ducks with her four-year-old grandson Mateus.

Do you have a Great Story?

If you enjoyed this collection of stories and feel you have an outrageous, funny, heartwarming or inspirational tale about animals that you would like to share, we would love to hear from you. Our only rules are that your story must feature some unusual, illuminating or humorous twist to it, and that it's a (mostly) true anecdote.

Although we've already published eight volumes in our humor series, we are still hoping to publish more books in the genre. So if you have a great story, please send it to us. You don't have to be a professional writer. We look forward to hearing from anybody who has a great yarn to spin.

To obtain more detailed submission guidelines, please visit Summit Studios online at:

www.summitstudios.biz

Please submit stories or story proposals by e-mail or snail mail to:

SUMMIT STUDIOS
3022 Washington Ave.
Victoria, British Columbia V9A 1P6

E-mail: submissions@summitstudios.biz

We look forward to hearing from you.

Acknowledgements

A very special thanks to my wife, Stacey, who has a love for great stories. Without her unconditional support and her belief in my dream to found a publishing company, it would not have been possible to share these stories with you.

A big thanks to Curtis Foreman for his help with the proofreading and to Kirk Seton for a fantastic book design. They are both top-notch professionals.

Thanks to my friends and family members who have offered their ideas, support, and critical feedback as this book has taken shape.

And finally, thanks to the many storytellers who have contributed their tales to this book. Their willingness to share means that we're all a little richer.

Other Titles by Matt Jackson

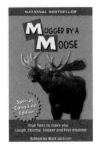

Mugged by a Moose

Edited by Matt Jackson

Is a bad day spent outside really better than a good day at the office? This collection of twenty-three short stories aims to answer that question.

> Humor/Travel • Softcover • 216 pages
> $19.95 • ISBN 9780973467130

Canadian Bestseller

"It's like Chicken Soup for the Funny Bone."
- The Kitchener-Waterloo Record

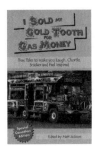

I Sold My Gold Tooth for Gas Money

Edited by Matt Jackson

Alternately laugh, cringe and giggle as twenty-six travel writers find themselves in some bizarre and unexpected situations.

> Humour/Travel • Softcover • 216 pages
> $19.95 • ISBN 9780973467147

Never Trust a Smiling Bear

Edited by Matt Jackson

The fifth volume in our bestselling humour series, where thirty-one writers serve up another helping of preposterous travel and outdoor tales.

Humour/Travel • Softcover • 216 pages
$19.95 • ISBN 9780973467185

The Canada Chronicles:
A Four-year Hitchhiking Odyssey

Written by Matt Jackson

Join the author on a four-year hitchhiking journey across Canada as he logs almost 30,000 kilometers, takes more than 25,000 photographs and meets hundreds of interesting characters from every corner of the country.

Adventure/Travel • Softcover
384 pages • 60 color photographs
$25.00 • ISBN 9780973467123

**Canadian Bestseller and Winner of the 2005 IPPY Award
for Best North American Travel Memoir!**

"Jackson's humor and charm shine throughout his storytelling."
- Canadian Geographic Magazine

A Beaver is Eating My Canoe

Edited by Matt Jackson

Another collection of wacky, funny, and inspiring tales from the far side of beyond, written by twenty-five free-spirited wanderers.

Humor/Travel • Softcover • 224 pages
$19.95 • ISBN 9780973467161

Canadian Bestseller

"Matt Jackson knows a funny travel story when he hears one."
- The Sarnia Observer

A Bear Stole My Fishing Boat

Edited by Matt Jackson

Traveling is not for the timid of heart. What can go wrong often does, as twenty-six travel-hardened writers relate in this book.

Humor/Travel • Softcover • 216 pages
$19.95 • ISBN 9780973467178

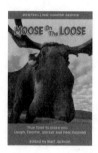

Moose on the Loose

Edited by Matt Jackson

The sixth volume in our bestselling travel and outdoor humor series, featuring twenty-six writers with stories that are outrageous, quirky, and downright hilarious.

Humour/Travel • Softcover • 224 pages
$19.95 • ISBN 9780986685606

Never Light a Match in the Outhouse

Edited by Matt Jackson

A collection of thirty-two funny stories from Cottage Country, and an ode to the shenanigans and mishaps that can happen there.

Humour/Travel • Softcover • 216 pages
$19.95 • ISBN 9780986685668

About Matt Jackson

A graduate of Wilfrid Laurier's Business Administration program in Waterloo, Canada, Matt Jackson was lured away from the corporate world by the thrill of adventure journalism while still a university student. He is now an author, editor, photojournalist and professional speaker, and is the president of Summit Studios, a publishing company specializing in books about travel and the outdoors.

Matt's first book, *The Canada Chronicles: A Four-year Hitchhiking Odyssey*, is a Canadian bestseller and won the IPPY award for best North American travel memoir in 2004. His work has also been featured in more than two dozen popular magazines including *Canadian Geographic, Backpacker, Canoe & Kayak, Explore,* and *BBC Wildlife*.

He lives with his wife Stacey and daughter Louise in Victoria, BC, where they spend as much time hiking and kayaking as possible.